Stories from the Raj:
Sahibs, Memsahibs and Others

Stories from the Raj:
Sahibs, Memsahibs and Others

Pran Nevile

INDIALOG PUBLICATIONS PVT. LTD.

For,
Gaurika, Siddharth and Tarini

Published in April 2004.

Indialog Publications Pvt. Ltd.
O - 22, Lajpat Nagar II
New Delhi - 110024
Ph.: 91-11-29839936/29830504
Fax: 91-11-29834798
www.indialogpublications.com
www.onepageclassic.com

Copyright © Pran Nevile
Cover Painting by F. Renaldi, Calcutta 1786

Picture Credits: On pages 10, 12, 13, 14, 16, 55, 75, 74, 77, 79, 80, 86, 88 from *Beyond the Veil: Indian Women in the Raj* by Pran Nevile; on pages 36, 43, 49, 51 from *Nautch Girls of India* by Pran Nevile; on pages 82, 84, 106, 174 Courtesy, British Library, London; on pages 121, 124, 129 from *Lahore: A Sentimental Journey*; on page 157 Courtesy, from the collection of Prince and Princess Sadruddin Aga Khan, Geneva; on page 163 Courtesy, Yale Center of British Art, New Haven, USA.

10 9 8 7 6 5 4 3 2 1

Printed at Chaman Offset Printers, Darya Ganj, New Delhi.

All rights reserved. No part of this book may be reproduced or utilized in any form or by any means, electronic or mechanical, including photocopying, recording or by any information storage or retrieval system, without the prior written permission of the publisher.

ISBN 81-87981-64-4

Contents

Section I

Sahibs and Bibis	10
The Oldest Profession	18
Memsahibs and the Indian Marriage Bazar	26
Nautch Nostalgia	36
Banning of an Indian Erotic Epic	49

Section II

India Through the Lens	56
Early Pictures of Indian Life	65
Portrayal of Indian Women by British Artists	74
Indian Paintings for the Sahibs	82

Section III

Fanny Parks – First Indophile Memsahib Traveller, Writer and Artist	90
Lola Montez – From Memsahib to Royal Mistress	99
From Farzana to Begum Joanna Sumroo	106

Section IV

Holi and Diwali – Two Queens of Festivals	114
Imperial Lahore – The Paris of the East	121
Pageantry of Princely India – A French View	133
First Imperial Durbar in Delhi (1877)	141

Section V

When Predictions Came True: The Brahmin Who Saw Tomorrow	150
Sahib's Fancy for the Hookah	157
The Great Rope and Other Tricks	163
Shikar and Animal Fights	172
From Arrack to Whisky	180

PREFACE

There is an old saying that old wine needs no bush. By the same token a book that is eminently readable may do without a preface. However, with everyone else who publishes a work, I share the common belief that a preface contains something which is not to be found in any other. I am, therefore, tempted to write this preface to introduce my book to the readers though I am aware of the fact that this page is seldom read.

Raj literature comprising journals, memoirs, diaries and travelogues by British scholars, travellers, officials and missionaries provides a rare insight and valuable information about the social and cultural scene in India. From these accounts, we learn about the lifestyle of the sahibs and memsahibs and also about their interaction with the natives of different classes. I have tried to cover some of the untold aspects of the Raj which are not usually dealt with in history books. The essence of history is not only to study the events but also what people thought and said about them.

There was a time when India was proclaimed to be the land of enchantments – the golden Orient, glittering in the best brilliance of sun and song – land of promise, and hope! Devoted to the life and times of common people, both sahibs and natives, the book seeks to amuse the readers with some tales of wine, woman and song. I do hope that when any description fails, the reader will find some diversion in looking at the true to life pictures of the contemporary scene that I have laboured to collect from different sources.

I wish to express my grateful thanks to Jehanara Wasi whose constant interest and encouragement made this book possible. I am also grateful to my wife, Savitri, who in spite of her poor health carried the burden of the family chores, leaving me free to pursue my chosen task. Finally, I am truly thankful to Chandana Dutta of Indialog Publications for the interest shown in my work.

New Delhi
April 2004

Pran Nevile

Section 1

Sahibs and Bibis

Imperial enterprise was a masculine affair. Deterred by the dangers of a long and tortuous voyage, few British women ventured to come to India. Further, the Original Charter of the East India Company forbade women on its posts.

British settlers first married widows and daughters of Portuguese Catholics, which did not find favour with the East India Company. So, towards the end of the 17th century, the Company copied the Portuguese practice and shipped batches of young women who were divided into "gentlewomen" and others for the marriage

Zenana scene - the bibi of an unknown protector by Thomas Daniell, c.1804

mart in India. As the demand for wives was far in excess of the supply, some women also took to prostitution, which was as a more lucrative vocation compared to marriage. For this "scandalous" behaviour, they were warned to mind their morals; otherwise they were to be fed only on bread and water till they were shipped back home. This experiment of importing women was abandoned by the Company in the 18th century, leaving its servants to find women for themselves.

Towards the end of the 18th century, there were only 250 European women in Calcutta while there were 4,000 men. Hence, both civilians and soldiers were encouraged – and even subsidised – by the Company to take native wives and mistresses.

It was a common practice for the sahibs to set up zenanas or keep Indian bibis. A bibi was an Indian mistress, a common law wife or a long-term consort of those Englishmen who could not afford to set up even a modest establishment in India. At times these Englishmen got married but there were insuperable difficulties in the way of a Christian wedding with a pagan.

Captain Thomas Williamson, who spent twenty years in the Company's service in India, in his famous guide book *East India Vade Mecum* (1810), justifies the practice of keeping Indian mistresses saying that it was far more economical than maintaining European wives. According to Williamson, "The attachment of many European gentlemen to their native mistresses is not to be described. An infatuation beyond all comparison prevails, causing every confidence, of whatever description, to be reposed in the sable queen of the harem."

In return many of these women, "have conducted themselves invariably in the most decorous manner and evinced the utmost fidelity, in every particular way, to their keepers; some have absolutely sacrificed property to no inconsiderable amount, and given up every pretension to caste; that is to admission among those of the same sect, or faith, braving the most bitter taunts, and the reproaches of their friends and relatives." He adds: "A woman under the protection of a European gentleman is counted not only among the natives, but even by his countrymen to be equally sacred, as though she were married to him – some are said to have passed twenty years or more, without the possibility for scandal to attach to their conduct."

Indian lady, perhaps the bibi of John Wombell, Lucknow, 1786 by Charles Smith

Until the arrival of Englishwomen in increasing numbers after the induction of the overland route via Egypt, the few Englishwomen who had come to India were mere adventuresses from the lower stock. In the opinion of one resident, these women were not "either in the education of intellect or heart what an intelligent, reflecting and cultivated man would select as his companion." They also got so intoxicated with their sudden elevation that many a sahib preferred an Indian bibi to these women.

Innes Munroe (1780-84) laments in his journal his countrymen's preference for the native to the white women. Further, the "upright, supple and slender well-rounded limbs" of Indian girls and their smooth skins of a bright chestnut colour added to their sexual attraction and no doubt turned many a male head. Samuel Brown, a company official, noted in his journal (c.1838) that "the native women were so amusingly playful, so anxious to please, that a person, accustomed to their society shrinks from the idea of encountering the whims, or yielding to the furies of an Englishwoman."

Sir Garnet Wolseley, who was in India just after the mutiny, confessed to his brother that he managed to console himself with a beautiful "Eastern princess" who "answered all the purposes of a wife without giving any of the bother." So he had no wish to be

William Palmer with his bibi Begum Faiz Baksh and children by F. Renaldi, Calcutta, c. 1786

caught in a European marriage to "some bitch" unless she was an heiress.

Dr. John Shortt, Company surgeon in Madras in the latter half of the 19th century, was charmed by the grace and beauty of Telugu girls. He wrote: "I have seen several of these girls in my professional capacity, while they lived as mistresses with European officers, and have been greatly surprised at their ladylike manner, modesty and gentleness, such beautiful small hands and little laper fingers, the ankles neatly turned, as to meet the admiration of the greatest connoisseur ... this is not to be wondered at that these girls were preferred to their own countrywomen."

There was an army colonel who even agreed to be circumscribed in order to get possession of a beautiful Muslim woman who imposed this condition for becoming his bibi. It sounds amusing to learn that an English editor of a local paper advised sahibs in 1783 to sleep with Indian women to keep themselves cool in the beastly summer of Calcutta. In fact, the Portuguese obtained a *firman* from the Mughal emperor Shah Jahan to keep Bengali women during summer to protect themselves from the heat of the Delta.

Resorting to bibis was not only a piece of erotic expediency, but these "sleeping dictionaries" also helped the sahibs to learn about the lifestyle, customs and manners besides the languages of India. Further, the bibi identified herself with the interests of her protector. She was an efficient housekeeper and a devoted nurse to her man if he fell ill. There was no stigma attached to these liaisons. At times, it was touching to see their mutual love and respect. The bibi was highly respected in society. Emma Roberts writes in her journal (1830) that: "Indian women, Hindu or Muslim, when they are attached to Englishmen confine themselves with singular dignity to the zenana of their protectors as if the marriage had taken place according to their own customs and ceremonies. They never go out of their houses and behave like lawful wives of a Muslim or Hindu of rank." The *bibikhana* or "ladyhouse" in a corner of the compound, separate from the main house, was an accepted feature of many a European bungalow.

The famous Sir Richard Burton writes in his autobiography (published by his wife in 1893) that Indian mistresses were a regular feature of the British military life. In 1840, there was hardly an officer in Baroda who was not more or less tied to a Hindu woman. These irregular unions were mostly temporary under an agreement and ceased when the regiment left the station. But in many cases, the bibis followed the regiment and lived with their protectors for years and bore their children as well.

Bibis and mistresses were left behind when the sahibs returned home. It was a moving sight to see them standing with their children on the riverbank, bidding farewell to their protectors as the vessel took them away.

But for the greater part of the 18th century,

Bibi of an unknown Englishman by F. Renaldi, Calcutta, 1787

the Company's officials had come to India to make a fortune through private trade and various other means, fair or foul. A favourite after-dinner toast of those days was "a lass and a lakh a day" – a normal objective for men who saw a lakh of rupees a worthwhile ambition and a bibi, a fitting companion. The post-Plassey English nabobs emulated the ostentatious lifestyle of the native princes and the Omrahs. For some of them a large zenana became a status symbol. Williamson cites the case of an elderly military man who derived solace from no less than sixteen mistresses of all sorts. He reckoned that the expenses of his mistresses were much less than maintaining an English wife.

The legendary David Ochterlony, the British Resident in Delhi (1803) popularly known as the "Loony Akhtar" lived like a royal prince. He used to take the air in the evening accompanied by thirteen Indian bibis riding elephants. William Frazer, the British Commissioner, who was murdered in 1835 in Delhi had seven Indian wives who lived together some distance away from Delhi. His favourite bibi was Sarwan, a Jat woman, whose "delicate beauty was beyond compare." Then there was Colonel John Collins nicknamed King Collins, the Resident at the Scindhias camp in early 19th century. He loved pomp and show and went everywhere accompanied by his zenana and a private artillery brigade. Contemporary observers have recorded that the plurality of bibis did not create any problems as they lived together with "tolerable cordiality."

The classic case is that of Job Charnock, the founder of the city of Calcutta (1696), who married Leela, a beautiful Brahmin girl after rescuing her from the funeral pyre of her husband where she was going to perform sati. Legend has it that Charnock was so much in love with Leela that he even got persuaded to live like a Hindu. Another Englishman Francis Day proved his deep attachment to his bibi by choosing a site for a fort in Madras in 1639, which was close to where she stayed.

Moreover, there was no shame attached to these liaisons. Even the Governor General Sir John Shore, and the Governor of Bombay and members of his council publicly kept native women. In fact, the will of Henry Littleton, a Company official, testifies to the virtues of his bibi, a Brahmin woman called Raja to whom he willed all his property and possessions. Then there is also the case

An Englishman's bibi by F. Renaldi, Dacca, 1789

of General John Pater who was so fond of his bibi that he built a church over her grave when the chaplain refused to bury her in the cemetery.

Contemporary paintings too depict the intimacy and closeness between the sahib and his bibi. William Hickey's touching account (1790s) of his attachment towards his bibi, Jemdanee, is as striking as the British artist Thomas Hickey's aesthetic portrait of this charming and dignified lady. Jemdanee, William Hickey writes, "lived with me, respected and admired by all friends for her extraordinary sprightliness and great humour. Unlike the women in Asia, she never secluded herself from the sight of strangers; on the contrary, she delighted in joining my male parties, cordially joining in the mirth which prevailed though never touching wine or spirits of any kind." He also extols her as "as gentle and affectionately attached a girl, as ever man was blessed with." Jemdanee was a great favourite with Hickey's friends who gave her presents and sent her affectionate messages.

Artists who came to India in the late 18th and early 19th centuries formed another group of Englishmen who also kept Indian bibis. They looked for patrons among the native princes and nawabs. They found it convenient to adopt local customs and preferred to live with Indian bibis. Tilly Kittle, the first British portrait painter was one of them and George Beechy, had two or possibly three bibis.

British artist Francesco Renaldi made quite a few portraits of Indian bibis, one of which was exhibited at the Royal Academy in 1791. Bibis in these portraits are shown as shy, modest, calm and composed. They appear in reflective moods, wearing shimmering costumes and elaborate jewellery.

However, in the third decade of the 19th century, the practice of keeping Indian bibis came to an end. With the introduction of the overland route as well as the introduction of steam ships, English girls started coming to India in large numbers to hunt for husbands. The practice of keeping bibis and native mistresses hence came to be frowned upon and Englishmen were advised to distance themselves from these native connections. On their part, the memsahibs too launched a full-scale campaign against bibidom. They spared no effort to abolish the bibi system as they considered it a threat to their position and also scandalous for the ruling class. Hence, thousands of contented bibis, loving wives and good mothers were driven from their homes. And after the mutiny of 1857, the institution of keeping bibis disappeared altogether.

The Oldest Profession

Indians have always sung praises of the "public woman." In her first incarnation she appears as Apsara, the celestial nymph who entertains the gods in the court of Indira, the God of the firmament. Apsaras are said to have sprung out of the ocean during *amrit manthan* (churning of the waters in the ocean) by the gods and the demons searching for the elixir of immortality.

Since neither the gods nor the demons accepted

A courtesan by Sir Charles D'oyley, Patna, c.1830

the apsaras as wives, they became common property, or *sumadatmajas* (daughters of pleasure) to be enjoyed both in heaven and on earth. Apsaras have been described as "tender maidens with the beauty of the rising moon, lotus eyes, lovely hips and thighs like plantain stems whose girdle bells tinkle as their slender waists bend beneath the burden of their swelling breasts."

Mythological tales also refer to apsaras as being commissioned by Indra to seduce the sages whose austere penance caused tremors in heaven. That is how, these tales go on to say, sage Vishwamitra succumbed to the charms of Menaka when Varuna, the Lord of wind, blew away her garments and Vishwamitra was captivated by the beauty of Menaka's bare body. On the other hand, some sages had acquired miraculous powers to summon apsaras from heaven to entertain their guests. In the *Ramayana*, there is a mention of sage Bhardwaj summoning apsaras to his hermitage for the amusement of Bharata and his warriors who had been sent to bring Rama back from exile.

It is said that apsaras were born on earth as devadasis to impart divine knowledge of dance and music to humans. As temple dancers, the devadasis were ceremoniously married to the deity in the shrine.

Patronised by kings and nobles, the devadasis appeared in different incarnations as *ganikas*, *nartakis*, and *rajdasis*, as appellations for the courtesans who carried on with the oldest profession. It was also not uncommon for kings to bestow special favours on their favourite courtesans and even acknowledge their relationship with these favourites.

The institution of courtesans formed an integral part of Indian culture and was a necessary element in the organisation of society. Courtesans enjoyed great esteem because of their learning and accomplishments – they were expected to be educated in sixty-four *kalas* (arts and sciences) including dancing, singing, acting, gymnastics and above all, dexterity in lovemaking.

The epics provide colourful descriptions of *ganikas* and their intimate connections with royal splendour. The *Puranas* state that the very sight of these women would bring good luck. Buddhist literature too testifies to the high esteem in which courtesans and pleasure girls were held in society. A *ganika* was treated as the ornament of civil life, "that lovely coloured, scented flower that the

Whorehouses in Dungarce near Bombay by T. Rowlandson, c.1800

city puts in its hair for all to see, when a festival or some other joyful event is being celebrated." Immortalised in romantic verses, poets describe her as "splendidly light, fair-hipped, young and tender and sweet to gaze on. Skilled in dance and song, practised in the service of love and gifted with the knowledge of the hearts' stirrings." The encounter between a courtesan and an ascetic is a recurring theme in Sanskrit literature. There are myriad accounts of the wealth of courtesans, their looks, their musical accomplishments and their religious charities.

By the time of Kautilya (200-300 B.C.) sexual love had been raised to the status of a true art form to be studied and taught by experts. Kautilya classifies public women in to different categories and describes their role in society, their rights, duties and privileges. He further lays down the principles of state control and organisation of prostitutes as well as the duties of *Ganikadhyaksa* or the Superintendent of the prostitutes. Kautilya uses the words *ganika, pratiganika, rupajiva, veshya, dasi, devadasi,* and *rupadasi* for courtesans and prostitutes. The *ganika* or the courtesan enjoyed a higher rank for her youth, beauty, and accomplishments. The prevailing concept then was that a woman of exceptional beauty and charm should be made a *Nagar Badhu* (city bride) who could be shared by men of taste, those from the nobility and poets. A notable example of this is Ambapali, the toast of Vaishali who mixed on equal terms with royalty and princes. Courtesans were also employed by kings to do espionage work and provide sexual hospitality to their guests and visiting princes.

The lawgivers enjoined that a courtesan must act honourably in her profession. There is an episode about a courtesan called Bindumati who astounded the great king Ashoka with the power of the Act of Truth by making the Ganges flow backwards and upstream. When the King asked her how she had attained these powers, Bindumati replied: "Whosoever, O King gives me gold – be he noble or a brahmin or a tradesman or a servant – I regard them all alike. Free alike from fawning and from dislike I do service to him who has bought me. This is the basis of the Act of Truth by the force of which I have turned the Ganges back."

From contemporary accounts we learn that the oldest profession prospered even in medieval India. Mughal rulers tried to impose some regulations and control but public women continued to enjoy the patronage of the nobles, princes and commoners. According to Nicolo Manucci the Kotwal in Lahore raised considerable revenue from the six thousand brothels in the city. In the South, Vijayanagar was famous for its elaborate organisation of brothels. There was also a well-established institution of devadasis in North India, which faded after the advent of Islam. Some of these devadasis indulged in prostitution with priests giving their profession a divine sanction.

Public women also enjoyed a great deal of popularity amongst Englishmen. They were not only accomplished in the art of love making but also seemed to enjoy sex for its own sake. Besides, their status carried no social stigma. William Foster, an English traveller in the early 17th century writes about a village in Gujarat allotted by the native ruler to a group of dancing women on the condition that they would raise their children in their own profession.

Later in the 18th century, we come across interesting accounts of white men patronising the local whores and boasting about their adventures. Many Englishmen were drawn by the bronze tint and shapely figures of the prostitutes. As the East India Company gained power and prestige in the 19th century, the oldest profession got more organised to cater to the physical needs of different classes of sahibs. Many Victorian men who would not openly maintain native mistresses and bibis, yielded to the sexual delights offered by the native courtesans and even recorded their pleasures

Nautch girls of Bombay, c. 1880

unashamedly. As did Edward Sellon, who arrived in India as a sixteen year old Company cadet in 1834: "Native women understand in perfection all the arts and wiles of love, are capable of gratifying any tastes and in face and figure they are unsurpassed by any woman in the world ... it is impossible to describe the enjoyment I experience in the arms of such syrens." Recalling his ten years of philandering, he mentions two kinds of prostitutes: one charging two rupees for her services, the other highly accomplished, five. He adds: "The 'fivers' are a very different set of people from their sisterhood in European countries; they do not drink, they are scrupulously cleanly in their persons, they are sumptuously dressed, they wear the most costly jewels in profusion, they are well educated and sing sweetly."

This oldest profession thrived in all Presidency towns and some brothel houses were staffed by European women recruited chiefly from South East Europe as well as by Chinese and Japanese girls. The government did take certain steps to register and supervise the prostitutes visited by Europeans as there were rumours of a white slave traffic between East Europe and India. There were also freelance operators in Bombay and Calcutta. Among the white women resident in India, those divorced by their husbands and unable to return home, ashamed of the disgrace they had brought upon themselves took to the flesh trade.

The Cursetji street in Bombay turned into a prominent centre for the well-off pleasure seekers keen to enjoy with foreign courtesans and sex workers. The missionaries protested against this licensed market of sin in the city. They started the "Midnight Mission" to patrol brothel areas shouting slogans like "be sure your sin will find you out." They paraded up and down the area accosting all men coming on to the street and even following them to their homes to note their names and addresses. This led to frequent brawls and the missionaries were assaulted both by the prostitutes and their white clients. At times the prostitutes would throw water or other nasty fluids on the missionaries from upper windows when they tried to deprive them of their clients. Eventually they were driven out by a court order, which stated that misguided missionaries could not be allowed to invade the streets at night and interfere with the rights and liberties of the public. All missionary zeal for imposing morality was of no avail and the sex trade in various forms continued to flourish until the end of the Raj.

The British authorities' concern for military efficiency forced

Nautch girls of Aurangabad, c. 1890

them to take an interest in the sex life of the soldiers due to incidences of VD, the most common disease in the British army. The soldiers came from the lower strata of society and lacked the moral fibre or intelligence needed for a life of continence. They were not allowed to marry because of economic considerations. Lal bazars (red light districts) functioned in all cantonments. Measures were taken to supervise the prostitutes visited by the British soldiers in order to prevent the spread of VD. The brothels in the cantonments were usually run by elderly madams who were paid fees from the regimental funds. Indian men were not permitted to enter the brothels used by the British soldiers. If caught, they were beaten up and thrown out. Sex was quite cheap; the standard rate in cantonments was one rupee for a sergeant, eight *annas* for a corporal and four for a private. There was an instance when the Commanding Officer of a regiment asked the cantonment magistrate or kotwal to provide for an adequate number of young and attractive women to be housed in the brothel area of the regiment bazar. He complained that he had only six women for four hundred men and calculated that he needed six more.

Nautch girls of UP, c. 1890

The missionaries and reformers of the purity movement protested over the official patronage of prostitution and demanded the eviction of prostitutes from cantonment areas. But the official view was that prostitution fulfilled a socially necessary function and their removal might lead to offences such as criminal assault, rape, etc. The military authorities considered Indian prostitutes in a positive light, as necessary to the satisfaction of the soldiers' physical needs. They also felt that it would be dangerous to deny men sexual outlets and put their masculinity at risk. They often emphasised that prostitutes were following their hereditary profession.

It is worth noting that the main military brothel in Lucknow cantonment was a spacious building with fifty-five rooms opening in a courtyard and run by a prosperous matron who would supply the workforce, take a percentage of their earnings, supervise them and come to their help in need so as to maintain her authority and control. The Indian press fully supported the official stand and according to one weekly paper: "Not to provide women for European soldiers who are drunk and mad with lust would be like letting beasts of prey." However, the English moralists' pressure continued and by the beginning of the 20th century, brothels were officially forbidden although Commanding Officers frequently made discreet but strictly unofficial arrangements for their men.

The British attitude to such social issues was governed by the imperatives of preserving their structure of imperial power. What a paradox – on the one hand the official authorities as a matter of policy provided necessary facilities for sexual relations between British soldiers and native women and on the other hand, they adopted strict measures to discourage sexual contact between British officials and native women. In both cases, the aim and objective were to presere the structure of power. In the case of a soldier, his masculinity had to be protected and his virile energies maintained and in the other case the social distance between the ruling elite and the natives had to be preserved.

Memsahibs and the Indian Marriage Bazar

Until the late 18th century very few British women ventured to come to India. It was a male dominated society where ladies played only a subsidiary role. These memsahibs did not share the scruples of later generations and showed due respect for native lifestyle and customs.

The ball for new arrivals by G. F. Atkinson, c.1856

They had no objection to the hookah and occasionally smoked it while the dames were on exhibition. The there were only two hundred and fifty European women in Bengal and its dependencies as against four thousand men. The cost of landing a European wife in Calcutta worked out to Rs. 5,000 – far beyond the means of ordinary Company officials. On the other hand, according to Captain Williamson's guidebook published in 1810, the expenses that had to be incurred on an Indian mistress worked out to Rs. 40 per month.

However, things did change and in that era of large families in England the only prospect for girls without dowry or physical beauty was spinsterhood. So more and more English women started coming to the great Indian marriage bazar. Moreover, as time passed and the British settlers acquired wealth and power, the memsahibs began arriving on the scene in search of rich husbands. Men who had amassed fortunes in India (called nabobs) were much sought after by the parents and guardians of marriageable daughters. Even as early as Robert Clive, girls just out from home were known as the "newly arrived angels" and there was great competition to get them ashore at Madras or to escort them from their carriages to the church in Calcutta.

As the 19th century rolled on, English ships brought regular cargoes of venturesome beauties bent on matrimony, growing into a social phenomenon called the "Fishing Fleet." With this influx of women, Edinburgh came to be called the "flesh market for the Indian marriage mart." London sent out supplies too. It was an age of quick marriages. The arrival of a cargo of young damsels was one of the exciting events for the waiting bachelors in India. To keep them chaste for the marriage market, unmarried women travelled under the care of chaperons, usually married women who were making the voyage to join their husbands. The age, height, manners, features and fashionable dresses of the young women became topics of conversation. On such occasions, the captains of the ships and other well-known ladies of the settlement would organise parties and the candidates for wifehood sat up, as it was called, for three or four nights in succession while the eligible bachelors, young and old rushed to try their luck. Matches were arranged on the spot while the dames were on exhibition.

The church on Sundays was also a recognised marriage bazar

A swarm of admirers hover around Miss C's carriage at Bandstand by G. F. Atkinson, c.1856

where the cargo of beauties appeared in splendour while the gallants waited on the steps of the church to greet them. They received proposals from all gentlemen, both known and not known. The greater part of the cargo was disposed of quickly. What was left of the "Fishing Fleet" sailed to the *mofussil* areas to scoop up husbands from the unmarried officials, soldiers, planters and businessmen. With such a multitude of wife-seekers, the woman had to be very ugly or over-ambitious not to find a catch and join the group of "Returned Empties," a term used for those returning to England without husbands.

The attention and court paid to these Englishwomen was astounding, as recorded by Sophia Goldbourne: "My smile was meaning and my articulation melody; in a word, mirrors are almost useless in Calcutta and self-adoration for your looks are reflected in the pleasures of every beholder and your claims to first rate distinction confirmed by all who approach you."

Poet Thomas Hood was so struck by this traffic that he satirises the ambitious husband hunters in a malicious poem which begins:

> *By Pa and Ma I'm daily told*
> *To marry now's my time,*

> *For though I'm very far from old,*
> *I'm rather in my prime.*
> *They say while we have any sun*
> *We ought to make our hay –*
> *And India has so hot a one*
> *I'm going to Bombay....*

And ends with:

> *My heart is full, my trunks as well,*
> *My mind and caps made up,*
> *My corsets shaped by Mrs Bell*
> *Are promised ere I sup;*
> *With boots and shoes, Riverta's best*
> *And dresses by Duce,*
> *And a Special Licence in my chest –*
> *I'm going to Bombay.*

Victor Jacquemont, a French botanist visiting India at the time was not much impressed by the English ladies he met in Calcutta and in other places. He wrote (1830): "Portionless girls who have not succeeded in getting married in England arrive here in cargoes for sale on honourable terms, I mean to young civil and military officers."

Another Frenchman, who served as an officer in the East India Company army, Captain Edouard Warren considered the parents' calculations of cost, risks and rewards rather sordid. He describes how the girls were advised by their aunts not to dance with anyone below the rank of a first class civilian or military officer who could provide three essential things for happiness of conjugal life in India: a massive silver teapot, a palanquin and a set of bearers to use by day, and a carriage in which to drive in the evening. Following such advice, the girl would foolishly refuse some really eligible wooers of whom she would not have dreamt of in England and succumb to the advances of some old nabob with spindle legs in whose mummy there was not a spark of heat and whose soul for the past twenty years had been concentrated on rupees.

In such a situation many of the girls became accomplished flirts. As long as the girl made a suitable catch in the end, flirting was accepted as a pleasant activity except when the girl overdid it. The young civilian was considered a prime catch – three hundred pounds a year dead or alive; the East India Company provided an allowance of three hundred pounds a year on marriage to a civilian and on his death a pension for the same amount was given to the widow.

Considering the prevailing circumstances, it is not surprising that many girls adopted a somewhat mercenary attitude to the whole matrimonial procedure, which is reflected in their letters and journals. Says one such letter:

"My dearest Maria, With respect to your request that I should tell you plainly what I think of these matrimonial schemes (for such they are, let people disguise them as they will) I never can impress upon you too strongly the folly and impropriety of your making such an attempt. Certainly, the very project itself is one of the utmost delicacy; for what is but running counter to all the dictates of that diffidence and native modesty for which English women have been so long held up as the perfect models?

"True it is that I am married; I have obtained that for which I came out to India – a husband; but I have lost what I left behind in my native country – happiness. Yet my husband is rich, as rich, or richer, than I could desire; but his health is ruined, as well as his temper, and he has taken me rather as a convenience than as a

Sale of English beauties in the East Indies by T. Rowlandson, c.1800

companion; and he plays the tyrant over me with as much severity as if I were one of the slaves that carry his palanquin ... What a state of things that, where the happiness of a wife depends upon the death of that man who should be the chief not the only source of her felicity. However such is the fact in India; wives are looking out with gratitude for the next mortality that may carry off their husbands, in order that they may return to England to live upon their jointures; they live a married life, an absolute misery, that they may enjoy a widowhood of a affluence and independence. This is no exaggeration I assure you.

"You know that, independent of others, there were thirty of us females on board the H –, who sailed upon the same speculation; we were of all ages, complexions and sizes, with little or nothing in common, but that we were single, and wished to get married. Some were absolutely old maids of the shrivelled and dry description, most of them above the age of fifty; while others were mere girls just freed from the tyranny of the dancing, music, and drawing masters at boarding schools, ignorant of almost everything that was useful, and educated merely to cover the surface of their mental deformity. I promise you, to me it was no slight penance to be exposed during the whole voyage to the half-sneering, satirical looks of the mates and guinea pigs, and it would have been intolerable, but for the good conduct and politeness of Captain S. He was a man of most gentlemanly deportment, but the involuntary compassion I fancied I sometimes discovered in him, was extremely irksome. However, we will suppose our voyage ended for nothing at all material happened, and that we are now safely landed at Calcutta.

"This place has many houses of entertainment of all descriptions, and the gaiety that prevails after the arrival of a fleet from England is astonishing. The town is filled with military and civil officers of all classes; and the first thing done after we have recovered our looks, is for the captains to give an entertainment, to which they issue general invitations; and everybody with the look and attendance of a gentleman, is at liberty to make his appearance. The speculative ladies, who have come out in the different ships, dress themselves with all the splendour they can assume, exhausting upon finery all the little stock of money they have brought out with them from Europe. This is in truth their last, or nearly their last stake, and they are determined to look and dance as divinely as possible.

"Such are the majority of the ladies; while the gentlemen are principally composed of those who have for some time resided in the country, and having realised fortunes, are determined to obtain wives with as little delay as possible. They are, as I have said, of all ranks, but generally of pale and squalid complexions, and suffering under the grievous infliction of liver complaints. A pretty prospect this for matrimonial happiness! Not a few are old and infirm, leaning upon sticks and crutches, and even supported about the apartment by their gorgeously dressed servants, for a display of all kinds of splendour on their part is no less of coyness or reluctance. In fact, this is the mode in which matches are generally made and if now and then one happy couple comes together, thousands are married with no hope of comfort and with a prospect merely of splendid misery. Generally speaking, in India, the officers make the best husbands, for they are frequently young and uninjured by the climate, and are the best disposed to attend to the wishes of their wives.

"This is called the Captain's Ball, and most frequently the greater part of the expectant ladies are disposed of there; it is really curious, but most melancholy, to see them ranged round the room, waiting with the utmost anxiety for offers, envy upon all who are more fortunate then themselves.

"If however, as is sometimes the case, a considerable number remain on hand, after the lapse of about three months, they unite in giving an entertainment at their own expense, to which all gentlemen are at liberty to go; and if they fail in this dernier resort, this forlorn hope, they must give up the attempt, and return to England."

Once a girl had been chosen it was time for the marriage. But the Governor General's licence to be married was necessary to constitute it a legal one. On the occasion of a marriage the officiating minister was accustomed to receiving as his fee between sixteen and twenty gold *mohurs*, and five gold *mohurs* for a baptism. No wonder that the chaplains were able to make such splendid fortunes in a short time.

Here is an extract from the *Lays of Ind* by Aliph Cheem, a collection of comic verse, which ran into several editions in the 19th century:

I do believe in dress and ease,
And fashionable dash.
I do believe in bright rupees,
And truly worship cash.

But I do believe that marrying,
An acting man is fudge;
And so do not fancy anything
Below a pucca judge.

I do believe that if I'm smart,
And do not lose my head
And cut that thing that's called the heart,
I may a fortune wed.

The Indian marriage market excited the imagination and ambition of generations of British girls. It was not unusual for a young girl to marry someone twice or even thrice her age. "India is a paradise of middle-aged gentlemen," wrote a lady from Madras in 1837. This was because young men in India "are thought nothing of being posted in remote areas to make or mar their fortunes" but at forty when they are "high in the service, rather yellow, and somewhat grey, they begin to be taken notice of, and called "young men."

Marriage notices such as the following were inserted in the Calcutta papers; "The marriage is announced of H. Meyer Esq. aged sixty-four to Miss Casina Coupers, a very accomplished young lady of sixteen after a courtship of five years." Some others read as: "A young man of genteel connections and a pleasing appearance, being desirous of providing himself with an amiable partner and agreeable companion for life, takes this opportunity to solicit the fair hand of a young and beautiful lady: personal accomplishments are absolutely necessary, though fortune will be no object, as he is on the point of taking a long and solitary journey to a distant and remote part of the country, and is anxiously solicitous to obtain a partner of his pleasures and soother of his woes. A line addressed to Mr. Atall, No. 100, Writers' Buildings, will meet with every possible attention and the greatest secrecy will not only be observed, but Mr. Atall will have the pleasure of giving due encouragement to their favour. Calcutta, The 21st November 1808."

Girls betrothed in England also came to India after years of waiting for their fiancés, but this did not always lead to happy reunions. Sometimes the man "no longer found the girl attractive" and dropped her, or if he had got married in the meantime, would convey his apologies and offer her all assistance in getting another husband. There were also occasions when the girl, after meeting someone on the voyage would have a change of heart and announce on arrival to the waiting aspirant that the engagement was off.

One also comes across some other amusing instances of matrimony. There was a Colonel in Madras who got married in January and, was presented with his firstborn in March! Another officer was cashiered for seducing an unmarried girl and then arranging her marriage with a brother officer. The most extraordinary case, however, was that of Sir Paul Joddrel, physician to the Nawab of Arcot (1790s). "He lived in Madras with his wife, a young niece by the name of Miss Cummings, and a child. After he had fixed the wedding of Miss Cummings with one Captain Charlise, it came to be known that the young one was Sir Paul's mistress, a

Rival candidates at Calcutta by James Moffat, c.1800

fact with which Lady Joddrel was well acquainted, and that the child was Sir Paul's by Miss C."

The demand for wives was so great that ladies who lost their husbands had no difficulty in replacing them. A widow got frequent proposals on the steps of the church after the burial of her husband. These speedy marriages were far from uncommon and there were even cases where a wife would engage herself to a suitor during her husband's illness.

One of the most famous much-married woman was Begum Johnson who got married at the age of twelve and took her fifth husband when she was nineteen. She died in 1812 at the age of 87 and was given a state funeral.

At times young wives with old husbands got involved in scandalous affairs with younger men and even eloped with them. Here is another verse from the *Lays of Ind*:

> Colonel White was over forty;
> Jane, his bride was seventeen;
> She was also very naughty
> For she loved a Captain Green!
>
> O Elders! Your hell has begun
> If at sixty you marry with youth,
> And can't be persuaded that fun
> May be coupled with virtue and truth!

As time passed more and more memsahibs appeared on the scene and started emerging as supporting stars in the great Imperial drama.

The great age of the memsahib, which began with the introduction of the overland route and the steamship in the 1830s, was fortified with the opening of the Suez Canal in 1869 and lasted until the end of the Raj. These memsahibs inculcated a feeling of racial superiority and brought little England to India. They enjoyed socialising with those of their own kind and were largely cut off from contact with real India.

Nautch Nostalgia

The word "nautch" is an Anglicised form of the Hindi/Urdu word *nach* derived from the Sanskrit *nritya* through the Prakrit *nachcha*, meaning dance. Nautch represented cultural interaction between the native and the early English settlers in India. Its professional exponent, the nautch girl, held the white sahib spellbound for nearly two centuries. "Delicate in person, soft in her features, perfect in form," she captivated the hearts of ordinary Englishmen by her grace and charm, enthralled the more

A British cadet watching a nautch during the Puja festival, Calcutta by Sir Charles D'oyly, c. 1810

sophisticated among them by her conversation and wit and enraptured the elite with her nautch which some of them found "superior to all the operas in the world."

Professional nautch girls and their performances have been described in numerous journals, travelogues, memoirs and diaries left by European visitors, missionaries, and civil and military officials. The fare provided by nautch girls fascinated most viewers and many a sahib was captivated by their seductive charm. The post-Plassey British nabobs who had made quick fortunes emulated the ostentatious lifestyle of native princes and omrahs. They even maintained their own troupes of nautch girls and musicians for the entertainment of their guests. A dinner in the community was usually followed by a nautch performance. So were other festive occasions, such as the celebration of a King Emperor's birthday and visits of dignitaries to civil and military stations. Nautch girls would also accompany the British army whenever it was on the move, entertaining the soldiers on the way. At times they were also engaged to welcome arriving guests on the highways. An army officer in his journal (1783) states that "he was met by his friend Major MacNeal who was preceded by a troupe of nautch girls. The latter encircled his palanquin, dancing until he entered the Major's house in Arcot."

So popular was this entertainment, especially with the soldiers, that nautch girls began to move en masse to British stations. Captain Williamson notes in his *Costumes and Customs of Modern India* (1813) that between the years 1778 and 1785, many outstanding dancing girls quit the cities, and retired to the cantonments, where they were received with open arms. Quite often, lonely men would send for nautch girls to entertain them in their own houses. Usually, groups of civilians or soldiers joined hands to hire nautch girls for an evening of amusement. They would often recite songs learnt from them and even translate them into popular ditties.

Nautch girls catered to a mixed society but it was men who got into the spirit of the nautch. Encouraged by the men's applause of *wah, wah* they would shed their stiff reserve and cool propriety, displaying their seductive charms. Captain Godfrey Charles Mundy (1832) in his journal mentions that "when European ladies attend a nautch, the dancing girls are warned beforehand and they only witness a graceful and sufficiently stupid display."

James Forbes in his *Oriental Memoirs* (1813) pays this

compliment to nautch girls: "They are extremely delicate in their person, soft and regular in their features, with a form of perfect symmetry, and although dedicated from infancy to this profession, they in general preserve a decency and modesty in their demeanour, which is more likely to allure than the shameless effrontery of similar characters in other countries."

The quality of the nautch and the class of nautch girls varied from place to place as did the reactions of the British spectators. In a typical early 19th century account, Captain Mundy describes a splendid nautch party held in honour of the Commander-in-Chief by the Company's Political Agent, Captain Wade in Ludhiana where forty-six nautch girls entertained the guests, only to be surpassed by the British Resident at Delhi who honoured the Commander-in-Chief with a performance by a hundred nautch girls.

In another account, nautch girls are portrayed as "pretty gazelle-eyed damsels arrayed in robes of sky-blue, crimson and gold in stately guise whose languishing glances stare brightly through their antimonial borders."

The nautch became a common form of entertainment in the mansions of the English merchants turned rulers in Bengal and other parts of India. In 1791, the Governor of Madras entertained the Nawab of Carnatic at a dinner with a nautch by girls of the devadasi community. This custom continued till the first half of the 19th century. Calcutta, the capital of the Raj, was known to be the stronghold of nautch. Wealthy Bengalis vied with one another in inviting famous nautch girls, even from faraway Lucknow and Delhi, for the entertainment of their European guests. The annual Durga Puja festival celebrated with great pomp was a special occasion for nautch parties. Invitations were issued through letters and cards couched in a florid style as well as through advertisements in the local press. At times, some influential babus succeeded in securing the presence of the Governor General, the Commander-in-Chief or other high dignitaries at these celebrations. Here is a news report from the Calcutta Gazette of 20th October, 1814:

"The Hindoo holidays of Durga Puja have begun. Many of the rich Hindoos vying with one another in expenses and profusion endeavour by the richness of their festivals to get a name amongst men. The principal days of entertainment are the 20th, 21st and 22nd; on which Nickee will warble her lovely ditties at the hospitable mansion of Raja Kishun Chand Roy ... Nor will the hall of Neel Mony Mullick resound less delightfully with the affecting strains of Ushoorun who for compass of voice and variety of note excels all the damsels of Hindostan. Misree whose graceful gestures would not hurt the practised eye of Parisot will lead the fairy dance on the boards of Joy Kishun Roy's happy dwelling ..."

Mrs. S.C. Bernos, a reputed artist who lived in Calcutta in the early 19th century, has invested nautch girls with a romantic aura. In her vivid description of a dance party held in Calcutta during the Puja festival, she observed:

A dancing woman of Bengal performing before a European family by Sir Charles D'oyly, c. 1810

"On entering the magnificent saloon, the eye is dazzled by a blaze of lights from splendid lustres, triple wall shades, chandle brass, etc., superb pier glasses, pictures, sofas, chairs, Turkey carpets, etc., adorn the splendid hall; these combined with the sounds of different kinds of music, both European and Indian, played all at the same time in different apartments; the noise of native tom-toms from another part of the house; the hum of human voices, the glittering dresses of the dancing girls, their slow and graceful movement; the rich dresses of the Rajah and his equally opulent Indian guests; the gay circle of European ladies and gentlemen, and the delicious scent of attar of roses and sandal which perfumes the saloon, strikes the stranger with amazement; but he fancies himself transported to some enchanted region, and the whole scene before him is but a fairy vision."

These splendid parties of nautch entertainment were covered by the local press, especially when dignitaries graced them with their presence. We find several absorbing accounts of nautch performances at Delhi, Bombay, Madras and other places. Observing that Delhi was the place where native dancing was to be seen in its perfection, Lieutenant Thomas Bacon (1831) gives a graphic description of a nautch held there in a spacious tent laid out for this purpose by Maharaja Hindu Rao:

"The tent was most glaringly lighted, *mussaulchis* or torch bearers stood here and there ready to attend to any person who might require them ... we had scarcely seated ourselves ere two of them made their appearance, floating into our presence, all tinsel coloured muslin and ornaments: they were followed by three musicians, and attended by a couple of *mussaulchis* who held their torches first to the face and then lower down as if showing off the charms of the dancers to the best advantage."

There is another fascinating description by Lieutenant Colonel Torrens (1860) of a nautch by Kashmiri girls in the picturesque Shalimar Gardens at Srinagar. The author was enchanted by the beauty of Shalimar, the queen of gardens, which he felt should be visited at night by the pale of moonlight when it is properly bedecked with torches, and crowned with lamps. Then "the proper thing to do is to give orders for a nautch at Shalimar." Apart from the beauty of the place, Torrens was enchanted with the dancing and singing of the charming Kashmiri nautch girls whom he considered "vastly superior" to what he had seen elsewhere. Another witness to a similar performance in Shalimar Gardens was a reputed professional artist, William Simpson, who was so much enthralled by the sight of nautch girls dancing by torchlight that he describes it as "the sweet delusion of a never to be forgotten night."

The immense popularity of the nautch can be judged by the fact that at times a dance performance would begin in the evening and last until daybreak. Among the prominent and most colourful British residents of Delhi at that time were Colonel James Skinner, known as Secunder Sahib and Sir David Ochterlony, nicknamed Loony Akhtar, who lived in royal style and held lavish nautch parties to entertain the English community. Colonel Skinner, a great patron of Delhi artists, would give away miniature paintings of nautch girls to his guests, sometimes of the very same dancers who were entertaining them.

Most of the descriptions by Europeans about nautch are,

Nautch Nostalgia • 41

A nautch girl singing to entertain memsahibs by Mrs. C. Belnos, c. 1820

however, repetitive but there is a singularly interesting one by Sir Charles Doyly from his long burlesque poem entitled *Tom Raw the Griffin* (1828):

> *See! how invitingly the creatures dance!*
> *What elegance and ease in every motion!*
> *Not as the ladies do at home, or France,*
> *So turbulent and full of strange Commotion;*
> *Of this our Indian fair have an odd notion;*
> *Their step is slow and measured – not a caper*
> *That lifts them from the ground, – but grave devotion*
> *To time, and suppleness of figure's taper,*
> *It is no doubt the modestest – at least on paper!*
>
> *Or how describe the graceful play of arms,*
> *Which, beautifully waving, as they move,*
> *Reveals, at every step, a thousand charms;*
> *Expressing terror, languishment, or love;*
> *While their dark, speaking eye, unceasing rove*
> *O'er all around – Few know the ditty's meaning:*
> *And – to speak truth, 'tis ten to twenty you've*
> *Not learnt the language, though – your dulness screening,*

> You shout applause, as if the tongue aufait you'd
> been in
>
> See the Circassian – 'tis a pleasing sight,
> With uplift arms her filmy veil is spread,
> Like a transparent canopy, and light
> As cobwebs on the lawn on which you tread,
> Rolling from side to side her airy head
> Swift as the agile roe's elastic bound;
> Then, in a giddy evolution led,
> Her full robes, whirling, gracefully around,
> She sinks amidst her sparkling drap'ry to the ground.

Captain Mundy found the dress of a nautch girl infinitely more decent than that of French and Italian figurines, but as a keen observer he noticed that "the upper portion of the costume ... is not quite so impervious to sight as a bodice of more opaque texture than muslin might render it."

From contemporary accounts one finds that "one of the most popular numbers in the repertoire of the nautch-girl was the *Kaharka nautch* or *Kuharwa*, the bearer's dance, which was usually performed before a male audience. While rendering it the nautch girl would tie a sash round her loins, through which she pulled up her gown and put another across her shoulders. Twisting a turban saucily round her head she would let her long black hair fall on her back and around her bosom and then dart forward with animated gestures, something of the nature of a Highland fling."

Another popular number considered graceful was the kite dance performed to the rhythm of a slow and expressive melody. The dancers would imitate in their gestures the movements of a person flying a kite. Commenting on this dance, one army officer observed that "the attitudes incident to this performance are most favourable to Indian grace and suppleness and the heavenward direction of the eyes displays these features, as doubtless my fair country women know, to the very best advantage." Among others, mention may be made of the snake dance where the nautch girl would put the ends of the dupatta in her mouth and mimic playing the gourd for charming a snake.

In South India, the dance tradition continued to be associated

Devadasis or dancing girls by Tilly Kettle, Madras, 1770

with the temple. While *kathak* flourished in North India, *dassi attam*, also referred to as *sadir nautch*, dominated the nautch scene in the South. It was far more than mere visible expression of a sung melody. It had a life of its own with a direct appeal to emotions. Often the dance was in itself the pantomime of a whole story. Dr. John Shortt in his account of *Dancing Girls of S. India* (1870) noted that their dance movements were marked by agility, ease and gracefulness, and the turning and twisting of their hands, eyes, face, features, and trunk were in complete harmony with their nimble steps whilst they beat time with their feet. Their dance was more feminine and suited to solo performances in temples and later in a court and at other public functions. There was greater emphasis on pure dance and *abhinaya* or expressions as they recited songs which were generally in praise of the gods but could also be interpreted in human terms for the benefit of their patrons.

The songs of nautch girls had as their themes either the amorous escapades in the lives of gods or conventional romantic tales, usually about the lover's yearning for the beloved. Until the end of the 19th century, songs in Persian were as popular as those in Hindi. The one

Persian ghazal by Hafiz which dominated the nautch scene for over a hundred years and invariably evoked roaring applause both from the natives and from the Europeans was *Tazah ba Tazah nu ba nu.* (Fresh and fresh, new and new). A mirthful melody in which the poet recommends applying the principles of fresh and new to all he does, whether in drinking, making friends, or making love. This finds mention in numerous foreign accounts of the nautch. There are even references comparing the singing style and the rendering of this ghazal by different reputed nautch girls of the day.

The nautch girls had a repertoire of songs, which became so popular with the sahibs that they got them translated into English verse. The Calcutta Gazette of June 9, 1808, carried a contribution from a correspondent who said, "Happening to attend a Cashmerian (sic) nautch a few nights ago, I was struck with the melody and effect of one of the native airs, which so much attracted my attention that I procured a copy and version of the song. The original is in the Cashmeree language, and the version has only the merit of being faithful:

> *Sleep! Sleep! let me sing thee to sleep,*
> *Sleep while my tresses o'ver thee*
> *Fall in fragrant caress.*
> *Sleep, for to watch thee reposing*
> *Is to me deep happiness.*
> *Sleep, sleep, let me sing thee to sleep.*
>
> *Wake! wake! let me kiss thee awake.*
> *Wake from thy dreams of beauty*
> *To the warmth of a real embrace.*
> *Wake from the chain of night's shadowy thrall.*
> *Wake! See the morn in my face!*
> *Wake, wake, let me kiss thee awake.*
>
> *Stay! stay! let me pray thee to stay.*
> *That the red light of returning day!*
> *Nay! 'tis not Sunset yet!*
> *'Tis but the gleam of his evening ray,*
> *That slants through the lattice still.*
> *Stay, stay, let me pray thee to stay!*

Until the middle of the 19th century, many Company officials were familiar with the Persian language and took interest in Persian poetry. There were even a few who would compose extempore couplets in Persian. These popular songs devoted to wine and women aroused romantic feelings and amorous desires among the audience. The visual display of human emotions served to enhance the appeal of the melodies as the spectators saw in them a reflection of their own hopes and aspirations. When a nautch girl addressed a patron with whom she had a liaison, the song would convey a meaningful message to him.

The nautch was thus an institution about which most sahibs had something to say. Exciting or boring, graceful or awkward, glamorous or dull, the opinions expressed were usually subjective. As Mrs. Mildred Archer, an authority on paintings by European artists in India during the Raj, says: "Judgement depended as much on who you were as on what you saw. Were you solemnly approaching the nautch as a serious part of Indian culture or were you accepting it as a frolicsome amusement which had beguiled countless Indians including the Mughal Emperors Akbar and Jehangir?"

As the 19th century wore on, the spread of English education brought in a new *petit bourgeois* class which, influenced by western ideas, got alienated from the art and cultural traditions of the country. This educated group was also swayed by the writings of some foreign observers who, without understanding the origin and nature of the Indian dance art and mistaking it for a representation of erotic temple sculptures, condemned it as "repulsive and immoral." They made no distinction between an accomplished professional nautch girl or a devadasi and a common prostitute, dubbing both as fallen women. The educated Indians, suffering from an inferiority complex, were overcome with a sense of shame about their own traditional arts.

By this time, the missionaries in their efforts to propagate the virtues of the Christian civilisation denounced Indian religious practices, social customs, and manners. The nautch institution in particular came under heavy attack as it was taken up as a moral issue. Some missionaries went to the extent of saying that nautch aroused anti-Christian feelings.

In their drive against nautch, the missionaries were also joined by a powerful group of educated Indian social reformers who, influenced by western ideas and Victorian moral values, had lost pride in their own cultural heritage. In 1892, they started an "anti-nautch" movement in Madras, which spread to other parts of the country as well. This movement was in a way inspired by the Madras Christian Literature Society which had launched virulent propaganda against nautch girls invited by the local gentry for a performance in honour of British dignitaries.

Among the missionaries, the crusade was led by Reverend J. Murdoch who launched a series of publications on Indian social reform in which his main target were nautch girls, who were condemned in extremely harsh terms. They were accused of impoverishing and ruining their patrons. The British official elite was urged to refrain from attending functions where nautch entertainment was provided. In an exclusive pamphlet addressed to English ladies, they were advised never to attend any such gathering themselves and to use all their influence to prevent their husbands from doing so.

Another publication entitled *Nautches – An Appeal to Educated Hindus* highlighted the evil effects of nautches ranging from loss of money, bodily weakness, and disease to injurious influence upon one's character.

The anti-nautch campaign gathered momentum with the support of the Indian press and the Social Purity Associations sponsored by the Purity movement in England for reform of public and private morals. One Miss Tennant even came all the way from England to persuade educated Indians to boycott their own dances. The Punjab Purity Association launched a forceful drive against nautches and published a booklet containing the opinions of eminent Punjabis vehemently condemning nautch girls. The booklet highlighted the denunciation of nautch by eminent reformer Keshub Chandra Sen who described a nautch girl as a "hideous woman ... Hell is in her eyes. In her breast is a vast ocean of poison. Round her comely waist dwell the furies of hell. Her hands are brandishing unseen daggers ever ready to strike unwary or wilful victims that fall in her way. Her blandishments are India's ruin. Alas! her smile is India's death."

Some of the agitators, who belonged to the Hindu Social Reform Association of Madras, appealed to the Governor of Madras and the Viceroy in 1893 to discourage what they said was a "pernicious" entertainment by declining to attend any function at which nautch

A nautch at the house of a Hindu Raja in Calcutta with British guests by Mrs. C Belnos, c.1820

girls were invited to perform. They also solicited the support of the Excellencies in their efforts to remove this evil practice on the ground that it had no sanction of religion, nor any claim to be considered as a national institution. However, both the Viceroy and the Governor, who had been present on several occasions on which nautches had been performed and had not found anything "which might in the remotest degree be considered improper," turned down their plea.

The Indian press, not satisfied with the replies of the Viceroy and the Governor, continued to plead for official support for the anti-nautch campaign. The *Madras Mail* urged Europeans to back the anti-nautch campaign by pointing out that "the Hindu social reformer is the product of our western education, and he must not be left to struggle on alone." However, Viceroy Lansdowne, who privately expressed his dislike for nautches, recorded: "I am not much inclined to surrender at discretion to these well-meaning but intolerant gentlemen."

The combined arguments of the reformers and the press failed to persuade the Government to take any action in the matter. However, the anti-nautch campaign continued in full blast and the National Social Conference at its meeting in Madras in 1894 adopted a resolution condemning nautches. The Bengali journal *Sanjivani* of December 8, assailed the Lieutenant Governor of Bengal, Sir Charles Elliot, for attending a nautch. Later, when Lord Curzon was approached by the reformers, he dismissed the issue as of little concern, not deserving any pronouncement or action on his part.

The reformers were, however, greatly encouraged by one Mrs. Marcus Fuller, wife of an English missionary in Bombay, who in her book *The Wrongs of Indian Womanhood*, published in 1900, strongly condemned the nautch institution and the practice of dedicating girls to temples. She reminded the reformers to keep knocking at the doors of the Viceregal Lodge till the Government took a policy decision against the viewing of nautch.

The persistent efforts of the reformers eventually bore fruit in 1905 when a decision was taken not to provide nautch entertainment at the reception that was held in honour of the Prince of Wales in Madras.

The coming of All India Radio and cinema provided opportunities for a few talented artists to practice their profession but most of them sank into oblivion. During the 1930s, there came an awakening when some lovers of the old performing arts of music and dance launched a vigorous drive to revive them. But their objective was to rescue it from the clutches of the "infamous" *tawaifs* and devadasis.

After independence, even All India Radio closed its doors to these professional women singers on the ground that "their private life was a public scandal." Thus the national Government became the guardian of public morality. The traditional performers of art were asked to prove their respectability – and that was possible only by quitting the profession and appearing in a new incarnation as chaste wives to be addressed as Devis and Begums in place of the traditional Bais.

And so honoured by royal lovers, rewarded by nawabs and nobles, patronised by the European elite, immortalised by poets and chroniclers, pursued by lovesick gallants, the Indian nautch girl, a symbol of glamour, grace and glory and the queen of performing arts, passed into the pages of history.

Banning of an Indian Erotic Epic

Apsaras, the divine courtesans who adorned the court of Indra, lord of the firmament, entertained the gods by dancing merrily to the accompaniment of music by Gandharvas. Urvashi, peer among the apsaras is said to have been born on earth as a devadasi who imparted divine knowledge of dance and music to human beings.

The devadasi institution was established all over India. The Chinese pilgrim Huein Tsang, who visited India in the 7th century, testified to the existence of a well-established institution of temple dancers. However, after the advent of Muslim rule, devadasis disappeared from the scene in North India but the practice

A devadasi with musicians by a Tanjore artist, c. 1800

continued in the South until the beginning of the 20th century.

In their heyday in the South, under the generous patronage of the Pallava, Chola, Pandya, and Nayaka Kings, devadasis were honoured with titles and gifts and their names are even mentioned in temple chronicles and inscriptions. They were trained from childhood in the arts of dance and music and were also taught classical literature in Sanskrit, Tamil, and Telegu.

Devadasis from Andhra Pradesh dominated the cultural scene in South India. A classic example of these devadasis is the celebrated courtesan, Muddupalani, who adorned the royal court of the Nayaka King of Tanjore, Partapsimha (1739-1763), a great patron and lover of music, literature, and the arts. He honoured and rewarded Muddupalani not only for her accomplishments in performing arts but also for her scholarly achievements as a learned poet well-versed in Telugu and Sanskrit. At that time, the Tanjore court was one of the few surviving Hindu patrons of the arts in India and attracted the best talent from other parts of the country.

Muddupalani's marvellous erotic epic *Radhika Santwanam* (Appeasing Radha) is a mid-18th century literary masterpiece and a gem of Telugu literature. But it was little known outside Andhra Pradesh. Credit goes to Susie Tharu and K. Lalita for bringing to light this great work through their excellent compilation, *Women writing in India – 600 B.C. to the Present* published in the early nineties. *Radhika Santwanam* consists of five hundred and eighty-four poems and is replete with the *shringar rasa* or erotic pleasure and presents the story of Radha and Krishna in a new light. It describes the story of Radha who brings up Ila Devi from childhood and then gives her in marriage to Krishna. There is a graphic account of Radha's detailed instructions to the young bride on the technique of lovemaking and the art of responding to Krishna's foreplay and motions. Then Radha, overtaken by grief at the separation from Krishna, taunts him in anger for neglecting her, as she is herself deeply attached to him.

Krishna then fondly appeases her with his divine loving embraces – the classic poem of Muddupalani takes its title from this episode. Later, there is an amusing narration of Radha's aggressive role and initiative in making love to Krishna when he is not in a sensual mood. Muddupalani is totally unconventional in her perception and treatment of the subject. She highlights a woman's dominating role and her active initiative in the game of love. It is the woman's gratification that takes precedence and forms the central theme of this great literary work. There is also an absorbing account of a young girl's coming of age and her maiden sexual experience. She finds faults with men for being unstable, impetuous, and unreliable.

Raja and the devadasis, Tanjore by a local artist, c.1800

Perhaps Muddupalani was inspired to write this book on the basis of her professional experience with men who sought her favours for love and romance. No wonder, this erotic epic became so controversial that it attracted even the Government's notice and censorship on moral grounds.

Hailing from a family of devadasis, Muddupalani speaks with pride about the literary achievements of her mother and grandmother who were both poets. In her autobiographical prologue, she proclaims her own eminence and popularity as a poet and scholar. She also describes with confidence and pride her physical beauty and charm, her gracious personality and her generous patronage of young artists and writers. She introduces herself with the following verse:

> *Which other woman of my kind has*
> *felicitated scholars with gifts of money?*
> *To which other woman of kind have*
> *epics been dedicated?*
> *Which other woman of my kind has*
> *won such acclaim in each of the arts?*
> *You are incomparable,*
> *Muddupalani among your kind.*

The first version of *Radha Santwanam* was published in 1887 and a record edition with a commentary by Venkatanarsu, an associate of the Orientalist lexicographer C. P. Brown, was brought out in 1907. This, however, omitted couplets of several poems as also Muddupalani's autobiographical prologue which tells readers about her accomplishments and eminence as a poet in the royal court. It was in 1910 that Nagaratnamma, a patron of the arts and a learned devadasi from Bangalore, not satisfied with the published version, decided to bring out the classic work in its original form. After extensive research, she finally succeeded in tracing the original palm leaf manuscript of this work and she published the new edition in 1910. Speaking about her determination to bring this masterpiece to the attention of the intelligentsia and general readers, she wrote in the preface that she could not resist the temptation of reading this book over and over again. She also highlights the fact that this epic brimming with *rasa* was not only written by a woman, but also by one born into her own community.

The following verse from *Radhika Santwanam* reveals Muddupalani's mastery of portraying visual images invoking the basic emotions of joy, excitement, sensual pleasure, and sexual bliss:

> *Move on her lips*
> *the tip of your tongue;*
> *do not scare her*
> *by biting hard,*
> *place on her cheeks*
> *a gentle kiss;*
> *do not scratch her*
> *with your sharp nails.*
> *Hold her nipple*
> *with your fingertips;*
> *do not scare her*
> *by squeezing it tight.*
> *Make love*
> *gradually;*
> *do not scare her*
> *by being aggressive*
> *I am a fool*

> to tell you all these.
> When you meet her
> and wage your war of love
> would you care of recall
> my "do's and dont's," Honey?

Translated by B. V. L. Narayanarow.
(*Women Writing in India* edited by Susie Tharu
and K. Lalita)

The above verse clearly shows that Muddupalani was an erudite scholar of Sanskrit literature and conversant with the writings of *shringar rasa* poets like Bhartrihari, Dandin, and Bilhana.

The publication of Muddupalani's classic work aroused lot of controversy and outright condemnation by contemporary social reformers. Many of them denounced it as obscene and labelled Muddupalani as a fallen woman.

A leading social reformer of Madras wrote that "many parts of the book are such that they should never be heard by a woman, let alone emerge from a woman's mouth. Using *shringar rasa* as an excuse Muddupalani shamelessly fills her poem with crude descriptions of sex."

This was also the time when the anti-nautch campaign was in full swing in South India. The Western-educated Indian reformers were alienated from the art and cultural traditions of the country and were influenced by the writings of the Madras Christian Literacy Society, which condemned devadasis in extremely harsh terms. The reformers even solicited the support of the Madras Governor and the Viceroy for the anti-nautch movement. This moral censorship dealt a deathblow to the traditional arts of dance and music and the devadasi institution.

As part of an Imperial design to justify their rule as a civilising mission, Indian cultural and traditional arts and customs were condemned as irrational and perverse. Not surprisingly, when the Government translator presented the English version of some objectionable parts of *Radhika Santwanam* to the authorities, the Government, already under pressure from the reformers, decided that the book would endanger the moral health of their Indian subjects and so banned it. Nagaratnamma gave a strong rejoinder to every criticism and put up a spirited defence but it was of no avail. There was a strong protest by the publishers who questioned the application of the Indian Penal Code "to ancient classics that have been in circulation for centuries." A conference of learned scholars also considered Government interference in this field as "inexpedient and undesirable and highly detrimental to the preservation and progress of Telugu literature." But the Government stuck to its decision and in 1911 all copies of the book were seized by the police and destroyed. Nagartanamma's publishers were charged with producing an obscene book.

It was only after independence in 1947 that the ban was withdrawn by the enlightened Chief Minister of Madras, T. Prakasan, who remarked that, "it had been a battle for pearls of great beauty to be replaced in the necklace of Telugu literature."

The publishers were also given permission to re-publish Nagaratnamma's edition of *Radhika Santwanam*, which was released again in 1952. What a boon it would be for lovers of literature not only in India but also abroad if this book is translated into English and other Indian languages.

Section 11

India Through The Lens

The camera appeared on the world scene in 1839 when Louis Daguerre unveiled his invention in Paris. It was immediately hailed for its "exact" image of reality. Made of silver, the first photographs were at once declared "mirrors of reality." Some even exclaimed that with the camera, "painting is dead." Places, events, and practically everything

American soldiers in India, 1943

in man's physical existence could now be brought into the camera's view. The camera immediately became popular and within less than a year it surfaced in Calcutta. By the 1870s, European commercial photographic firms had set up their shops in every large city of India.

Indians took up photography as a lucrative professional enterprise and as a fashionable hobby. In the early years, Indian professional artists, especially portrait painters, willingly used photographs as painting aids but in due course many of them switched professions and became photographers. Photography rapidly replaced painting, at least in respect of portraiture. Photography also received Government patronage and the camera replaced the draftsman in recording historic monuments and edifices. The Government also subsidised photographers for recording military expeditions and public works projects.

The early European commercial photography firms took over the tradition of the work done by professional British artists like Thomas and William Daniells who had come to India in the late 18th century and who specialised in views of the picturesque and the exotic. India, the great Eastern wonderland, with its bewildering diversity of people, its magnificent monuments of past grandeur, its gorgeous palaces, wonderful temples, the beauty and serenity of its landscape and the fascinating flora and fauna provided rich material for photographers.

The best known European firms of photographers in India in those days included M/s Bourne and Shepherd, Johnston and Hoffman, T. A. Rust, John Burke, Nickholos & Co. and Barton & Son. They produced a series of photographs on many views of India. The camera recorded India in the 19th century but the photographers projected India according to their own perception of what they saw, felt, and thought about the land and its civilisation. They also produced photographs of the picturesque façade of the Empire, the pomp and show of the grand durbars – the glittering rituals of the Raj.

Architectural photography was dominated by famous monuments – The Taj Mahal, the Benaras ghats, and Tanjore temples. The native people of India of different castes, classes and ethnic groups, and also various professionals with their colourful costumes formed an interesting subject for some photographers.

Jama Masjid, stereograph, c.1890

They were, however, restricted to photographing only the male subjects. When it came to Indian women, they faced the same problem faced by early British professional artists. They had to depend on nautch girls, courtesans, others from the countryside and tribal women who were free from the purdah. The women of upper classes, from both Hindu and Muslim communities, would not face the camera wielded by a man because of societal restrictions.

There was a rare exception when a few upper class women were persuaded to expose themselves to a cameraman as a special favour to honour and gratify Queen Victoria, who, on the assumption of direct sovereignty of India in 1859 wanted the photographs of her Indian subjects – men and women of various castes and professions. Considering the market potential in this field, one Mrs. Garrick set up a studio in Calcutta and specialised in photographing women.

The renowned Indian photographer of the 19th century, Raja Deen Dayal also employed a lady to photograph women in purdah. In due course, some other photographers also employed women to visit the zenanas and photograph ladies in their quarters.

Like the painters earlier, Indian photographers flocked to princely courts for their patronage. In addition to portraits of the princes and their family members, they also covered festive events like weddings and other social occasions. Some Indian princes appointed official photographers in their courts.

Indian photographers, while using the same camera equipment

as was being used elsewhere, produced a different imagery. They called themselves artists/photographers and clicked photographs that emulated the style and form found in Indian paintings and were in tune with aesthetic traditions. It is now an established fact that like a painter, the photographer can also stamp his individuality on his work. Indian photographers of those times who attempted to do this were truly remarkable. However, they lacked the expertise as well as the resources to undertake landscape photography. It was left to European firms to produce photographic prints and mounted photographs covering a variety of subjects on popular demand.

Travellers and visitors to India at that time did not yet carry personal cameras and invariably bought photographs of the Indian panorama as souvenirs and mementoes from the market dominated by European firms.

The first monumental book with photographic illustrations, *Glimpses of India* (with over five hundred pictures) was published in 1896. Edited by J.H. Fourneaux and commended by Mark Twain, the book was hailed as a pioneering work, highlighting the fact that "no work of painting alone can convey such a realistic conception of those places as the absolutely accurate reproductions

A sweets shop in Delhi, c.1880

Elephants toe a carriage in Delhi during the great durbar, 1903

of the photographs contained in this volume." It was also mentioned that these photographs were specially prepared by leading European commercial photographers of Calcutta and Bombay and also by Lala Deen Dayal & Sons, Secunderabad.

During the last quarter of the 19th century, traditional artists were struggling hard to survive the onslaught of the camera. Earlier they used to make sets of colourful paintings of native people of different occupations in their exotic costumes, their festivals and rituals as well as the local scenery with its typical flora and fauna. Now, with commercial photographs, these artists lost their clientele. They were compelled to switch professions and many of them became photographers. Some of them developed and introduced the novelty of painting photographs.

Early photographs of the late 19th century though yellowing with age, show the high quality of the work executed by photographers, endowed as it was with inherent Indian aesthetic traditions. Black and white pictures, however, were not quite attractive and lacked the dazzling impact of the brightly-hued ones. The latter appealed to the rich and famous who wanted colour pictures to show the glamour and grandeur of their wealth and power. It was also felt that India, with its vast diversity of people and the beauty of its scenery, would be robbed of colour if shown in black and white. For a true picture of the country – especially for those living abroad and who did not have the opportunity of visiting India – the land and its people had to be shown in colour as it provided extra information about the subject in its descriptive content.

The art of hand-colouring black and white images is as old as photography. The technique was developed in order to create a realistic appearance of the subject. The Indian artist-photographers, however, produced another realistic kind of image – the painted picture that became immensely popular in the late 19th and early 20th centuries. It was considered the most natural photograph and also the most appealing. This picture was usually partially painted but on some occasions it was completely painted over leaving little trace of the original lens image. All the same, the final product revealed the artist-photographer's rich tradition of artistry and workmanship and was also most appealing.

A photographer used colour in an interpretative way to produce fresh shapes, forms, and expressions about the subject. We react subjectively to colour as it has the potential to create and change a mood. The artist-photographer achieved the desired result through the dominance of a particular shade or tint over all others.

A painted picture called for the skills of a team of artists. One was responsible for retouching the negative with a shade of red or

The Taj Mahal, stereograph, c.1890

pink in order to wipe out the dark areas of the picture. The second undertook the finishing work on the photo-print with crayon and pumice in order to soften the light and shade effects. The third painted the background with water colours while the fourth expert outlined figures in a photographic print giving them a silhouette effect. The last man of the team was the oil painter who supplied the final magic to the picture. The combination of hand painting and photography presented a novel picture with a brilliant new range of tones. Rooted in Indian skills and perceptions, these pictures developed into a novelty totally Indian.

As a creative technique, hand painting offered unlimited scope in adding emphasis to a picture. The artist would often change the background scene by adding or excluding certain decorative effects, items of furniture or changing a facial expression of the subject in order to show authority, grace or kindness as desired by the patron.

Raja Deen Dayal, the renowned Indian photographer who was appointed by Queen Victoria as one of her official photographers could photograph both in European and Indian styles. Many of his Indian style photographs were retouched, painted and finished to meet the increasing demand for bright painted pictures from the aristocracy. Commercial photographers painted photographs of Indian people of different classes and professions attired in colourful costumes. These were used not only as illustrations in books and in travel literature but also as picture cards for tourists. These photographs were more than beautiful objects since they represented a tradition and an expressive form for Indian artist photographers at that time.

The novelty of painted photographs, however, did not find favour with Europeans who considered it a device to cover up the flaws in a photograph or hide the ineptness of the photographer. As the 20th century rolled on, growing influences of Western education and ideas brought about a significant change in people's outlook and tastes. The painted photograph eventually lost its popularity with the elite and finally vanished from the scene.

Another novelty conceived in the infant years of photography appeared in the shape of the stereograph, also known as the stereogram, a three-dimensional picture. Stereography, first described in 1832 by English physicist Charles Wheatstone as uniquely photographic, was perfected between 1850 and 1856.

Stereography is a double photograph of the same subject produced by juxtaposing two views taken simultaneously but from different points separated horizontally by 2 inches (6 cm), approximately the normal distance between the human eyes.

It presents a 3-D solid image when seen though a binocular viewer of the stereoscope. The principle of stereoscopic vision is based on the fact that the two eyes perceive slightly different images when directed at any given object. The two images are fused in the brain to produce the sensations of relief and perception.

As 3-D photography became a rampant craze, the stereoscope emerged as one of the most popular diversions of the Victorian era. From 1860 till about 1920, a stereo viewer was as ubiquitous in British and American homes as the TV is today. Even in India, the affluent class in major cities took pride in the possession of a stereoscope with a collection of stereo cards displaying views of Europe and America. Through the illusion of three dimensions, people were not only entertained but also enlightened by stereographs of every description – geography, history, religion, and customs and manners of the people of distant lands.

An American woman is served tea in Lucknow, c.1890

The credit for the extensive popularity of stereography goes to the American Underwood brothers who with aggressive and novel marketing techniques set up one of the most successful businesses in the history of stereography. They packed their merchandise in boxes, which looked like books and contained, besides cards, a guide book full of information on the subject of the set with a map showing the location of the view and its historical background. By 1901 the Underwood Company was almost the global leader in the business, manufacturing twenty-three thousand stereo views per month and three hundred thousand stereoscopes annually.

The Keystone View Company was another major producer of stereo views and when Underwood diversified into other areas of commercial photography, it sold off its vast holdings of stereo negatives to Keystone. After 1920, Keystone was the only important manufacturer of photographic stereo views and stereoscope in the world.

Most of the stereographs carry the imprints of American companies like Underwood Publishers and the Keystone View Company. Many American photographers had begun visiting India from the late 19th century and took stereo pictures of the country's landscape and people. They also acquired stereo negatives from local European commercial photographers for their boxed sets (on different aspects of Indian historical and geographical studies) for worldwide distribution.

The life of stereographs, however, was less than a century, roughly from 1850 to 1930. With the advent of cinema, radio and TV, the popularity of stereographs soon faded and after 1930 the stereoscope and the picture cards practically vanished from the scene.

The US Library of Congress in perhaps the only repository of a vast collection of stereographs dating back to the 1860s. This rare collection presents a reservoir of information about the life and times of a bygone era through the eyes of its cameramen. So much has changed the world over during the last one hundred years that these stereo views have already become a sort of heritage item.

Early Pictures of Indian Life

The last quarter of the 18th century witnessed a remarkable flowering of British interest in Indian history, literature, antiquities, and the customs and manners of its people. Lured by the prospects of fame and fortune, a number of British artists began arriving in India. Until then there had practically been no visual record of the Indian scene.

Palace of the Lal Bagh at Seringapatnam by Charles Gold, c.1790

Now the Englishmen and women in India were struck by the bewildering diversity of its people, their colourful costumes, unusual occupations, novel means of transport, strange musical instruments, and lively fairs and festivals. They were curious to understand the people around them, but no book depicting Indians and their way of life had yet been published. British artists working in India devoted themselves to landscape painting, which had a ready market, or to painting portraits of the ruling elite and the princes. On the other hand, the prevailing delight in the picturesque led to a growing demand for pictures of trades and occupations, customs and manners of the people, and their costumes.

It was in 1794 that Francois Baltazar Solvyns, a French artist married to an English lady living in Calcutta, proficient neither in landscape painting nor portraiture, decided to apply his talents to the neglected field of depicting Indian people and their way of life. Solvyns came to India to seek a fortune as an artist in 1791 after training in Antwerp as a painter, sketcher, and an engraver. Within a short period, he came under the spell of India and praised the country in superlative terms. He even learnt Hindi and enjoyed the company of learned pundits and brahmins. In the beginning, he took up odd jobs with the East India Company for ceremonial decorations and the cleaning and restoration of paintings. He also made a living by giving lessons in painting and drawing, but his steady source of income was the ornamentation of coaches and palanquins.

Solvyns was easily the first professional artist to undertake a comprehensive study of Indian communities, costumes, and customs. Noticing the keen British interest in this field, he launched on a grandiose project to produce two hundred and fifty coloured etchings descriptive of the manner, customs, character, dress and religious costumes of the "Hindoos." He was encouraged and supported in this gigantic task by Sir William Jones, the renowned Orientalist and founder of the Royal Asiatic Society in Calcutta. Being the first venture of its kind, it brought in sufficient subscriptions that enabled Solvyns to proceed with his project. He recorded that his pictures of the Indian scene would be particularly interesting to those who had resided for many years in India and, upon their retreat to their native country, would help them recall the occurrences of their youth and scenes formerly familiar to them.

Nautch by Hindu dancing girls by B. Solvyns, c.1800

Solvyns began drawing his subjects from real life which included men and women of every possible caste or calling, from the high caste brahmin to the milkmaid. He portrayed many servants with their specific duties. He also drew pictures of the colourful Indian festivals, ascetics, and various forms of transport – palanquins, sedan chairs, and carts drawn by bullocks or horses. He sketched the boats on the river and in the harbour, both pleasure boats and boats of lading, different kinds of pipes for smoking, and a variety of musical instruments.

After completing these drawings, Solvyns made etchings from them and coloured them by hand. He completed his project in 1796 and continued for another eight years to work on further sets ordered by his subscribers. Of these drawings, two hundred and forty-nine are held in the collections of the Victoria and Albert Museum in London. Solvyns' work was published in Calcutta in 1799. It is not known whether Solvyns did all the work himself or he employed local native artists to assist him in this huge task. It is noticed, however, that over the years, there were distinct variations in the finish – differences in colouring and mounting resulting in every set with a quality of its own.

A Moorish Fakir, decorated for the Muharram festival, Trichinopoly by Charles Gold, c.1790

However, despite all his hard work, the whole project was a financial failure. The reasons for Solvyns' failure find mention in the *Calcutta Gazette*'s obituary notice of May 18, 1826. "His sketches," it noted, "though not very picturesque, are very faithful delineations, and he must have been a man of very laborious and observant research. The engravings executed by himself and published in Calcutta are very rude." Judged by contemporary European standards they were dubbed monotonous and unattractive. Solvyns' engravings with rough hatching, fuzzy shading and dull colouring were not much appreciated by the British public who were by now used to aquatints of excellent quality with soft colouring and subtle gradation of tone. But the subjects were of great historical value and his sketches faithful representations of what he saw. That Solvyns' project was a well-conceived pioneering work of its own kind was proven by the success of a pirated edition of sixty prints of redrawn Solvyns' subjects brought out by a London publisher, Edward Orme, as *Costume of Hindostan*. But Solvyns gained nothing out of it and was able to continue with his work thanks to the financial support of his English wife with private means.

Solvyns left India for France in 1804. He resumed his work in Paris and produced a French folio edition of two hundred and eighty-eight plates, *Les Hindous*, published in Paris between 1808 and 1812 in four large volumes. The accompanying descriptive text with each plate gives detailed information about the subjects depicted. In the introduction to *Les Hindous*, Solvyns describes Hindoostan (sic) as "the Paradise of the World with its fertile soil, agreeable climate and the abundance of everything necessary to the wants or even to the pleasure of life." He refers to the "Hindoos" (sic) as a "portion of mankind exempt from ambition, from vanity, from curiosity, satisfied in the enjoyment of what nature bestowed, and possessing in their mild and calm disposition that happiness which they themselves had pursued so long in vain, through the mazes of philosophy and science."

However, the French edition of his work was also not a financial success. Later he did not even succeed in organising a lottery of his drawings and paintings. He subsequently died in 1824.

As an artist Solvyns set a new trend later visible in Company scheme paintings. Also, his work is of great historic value and, with its accompanying descriptions, constitutes the first ethnographic survey of India. He was easily the first European to provide a systematic ranking of castes. Yet art historians and anthropologists have taken little note of Solvyns' pioneering work and his portrayal of the Indian social scene in the late 18th century.

Though Solvyns' venture at first sight seems to be a financial failure, it is interesting to observe the tremendous influence that his work had on the fortunes of Indian painters who were gradually moving to Calcutta and other British stations in the Bengal Presidency such as Patna, Chapra, and Murshidabad. With the decline of Indian patronage after the collapse of the Mughal empire, Indian artists were eagerly looking for the patronage of the new rulers – the British. They were skilful and clever enough to adapt their painting style to meet the tastes and requirements of the new masters. They were also in search of subjects that would appeal to their new clients. They noticed a growing demand for sets of paintings depicting subjects covered by Solvyns such as castes, trades, occupations, methods of transport, religious ceremonies, and festivals.

In Solvyns' sketches they found the best guide and their works found a ready market and they were well rewarded for their marvellous paintings in water colour on imported paper. Throughout the first half of the 19th century, Indian painters produced pictures strongly reminiscent of Solvyns' plates. They adopted similar types of compositions and produced sets depicting specific subjects – which were sometimes embellished with pictures of local rulers and their court scenes.

Smoking the hookah over a game of chess, Coromandal Coast by Charles Gold, c.1790

As regards the pictures of life in South India, we have to explore the visual record left by the British amateur artists of the period. Most professional artists landed in Madras as it was the first port of call for the English ships, and a few like Tilly Kettle, George Willison, Thomas Hickey, and George Chinnery prospered there. For the rest it was the city of Calcutta that offered official patronage and opportunities to make their fortunes.

Towards the close of the 18th century, a new generation of young, middle-class Englishmen with good education came to India for employment by the East India Company. This was a period in England when painting and sketching were part of a liberal education and it was a common practice for young boys and girls to receive instructions in drawing in schools or at home. Hence, many of the new Company officials were well equipped in drawing. Not only were they competent with pencil, pen, and brush but they regarded sketching and painting as a valuable accomplishment.

Some of these amateur artists were highly gifted and also skilled water colourists and their work was in no way inferior to that of the professionals. In fact, before the age of the camera, many of their sketches were used by publishers to illustrate books so as to gratify the British passion for pictures. Captain Charles Gold, who joined the East India Company army as a captain in 1776 belonged to that distinguished class of amateur artists who were dedicated and sincere enough to learn about the country and its people. He was indeed the first to make a pictorial study of the local people of different castes and classes in South India. Just as Solvyns took his subjects from Bengal, Gold presented a companion picture of South India. Scenery, costumes, occupations, and customs blended into his sketches with utmost skill. Sensitive to the sights and smells and to the colours and shapes of his environment, Gold depicted his subjects with remarkable fidelity and astonishing detail.

Like Solvyns, Gold seems to have realised that there was no book depicting native people of different castes and classes and so he began work independently on the Coromandel Coast where he was posted during the British campaign against Tipu Sultan.

While he was travelling with a detachment of the Royal Artillery between 1791 and 1798, Gold made drawings of various local people he met on the way. Fifty of these drawings were reproduced as aquatints in *Oriental Drawings* published in London in 1806. Most of Gold's drawings are remarkable for their spontaneity, directness of observation, a kindly feeling for Indians and at times for their lively humour. An army officer, not a professional artist, he tells us that "not being enabled from his professional duties, to go in search of the extraordinary subjects with which it (India) so eminently abounds," he was "necessitated to take them as they occurred." Gold adds that he "allowed none to pass his quarter, without an invitation to walk in, which they always accepted, and most readily permitted him to draw their portraits." He assured that the "dress are minutely attended to and the characters strictly preserved."

Gold's drawings range from a dramatic dust storm to a marriage procession, to an ascetic, a wandering minstrel, villagers going about their work, women pounding rice, barbers, jugglers and even a pious brahmin making offerings to the monkey god Hanuman in a temple in Madras. Such scenes and subjects were so unfamiliar to the English that Gold gave a comprehensive descriptive account explaining the sketches. These accounts displayed Gold's knowledge and his extensive study of Indian texts. With regard to his sketch of Hanuman, he noted, "On visiting the Pagoda (temple) ... we were permitted to view some of these curiosities ... I had only time to sketch the one nearest the door, which was in the best light and from his countenance he appeared to be Hanuman, immortalised for the services he performed under the God Rama at the conquest of Ceylon. He is on a stage, in the exact attitude of the original, and represented as accepting an offering of fruits."

Hindu festivals and religious ceremonies aroused great interest among the British and Gold provided illuminating comments and observations on these topics with vivid paintings. His discerning eye was able to identify the Vaishnavites from the Shaivites and he painted many religious and festive scenes portraying them.

The British were also fascinated by jugglers and snake charmers and Gold was no different. He left behind interesting accounts of Indian snakes and reptiles and also wrote about the origin and practice of serpent worship in India. Impressed by the performance of snake charmers, Gold was led to believe in the force of music, which he thought was responsible for luring snakes out of their lairs. Yet another subject that intrigued Gold was the wandering

The howdah belonging to the Governor General by William Simpson, c. 1860

mendicant or *fakir* and he wrote and painted extensively different types of *fakirs*, their religious habits, their backgrounds, rituals, and practices. He was also inspired by the sets of pictures sold by Indian artists portraying men and women of various castes and occupations. Gold even reproduced pictures of a lame beggar and his family made by one Tanjore artist.

The vast body of visual material created by Baltazar Solvyns and Charles Gold before the age of the camera is truly an eye opener as regards our past and serves as a rich reminder of our culture, customs, and heritage. These true to life sketches and drawings of Indian social and cultural scene in the 18th century are of great historical value and bring to life the customs, manner, and the pattern of living of the people of different classes in different parts of India. These valuable records add a new dimension to the contemporary Raj literature comprising memories, diaries, travelogues and journals left behind by scholars, travellers and British Company Officials.

Portrayal of Indian Women by British Artists

Indian women have always been considered among the most beautiful in the world and their charms have been celebrated by poets and artists throughout the ages. Until the middle of the 18th century there was no visual record of Indian people based on first-hand observations. Travellers carried home tales of kings and their hordes of dusky beauties, dripping with pearls and diamonds in gauzy veils, languishing in the harems or reclining in marble palaces or in royal gardens which bore little relation to reality.

There is reference in literature to portraits of women but none has been preserved from ancient times. Images of women are, however, a recurring

Shahzada Begum, a woman of rank at Delhi by William Sampson, c. 1860 (from the John Goelet collection)

theme with the miniature painters of Mughal courts and Rajput kingdoms. These paintings were not true to life representation of women but rather highlighted their elusive nature and the exotic and almost unattainable beauty the ideal woman was conceived to possess. The artists applied their talent more to give a visual expression to, and depict the essence of, human sentiments and emotions of joy, ecstasy, and anguish.

British artists began arriving in India from the 1760s

A Bengali woman descending the steps of a well by Fredrick W. A, De Fabeck, Calcutta, c. 1860

onwards. Most of them, lured by the prospect of fame and fortune, concentrated on making portraits of British elite and native princes, landscape paintings, or pictures of Imperial interest commissioned by the East India Company. However, there were some, both professional and amateur, who applied their talents to depicting the real India and its exotic people, especially native women. Historian Robert Orme (1750) had already aroused their curiosity with his remarks that "nature seems to have showered beauty on the fairer sex throughout Indostan (sic) with a more lavish hand than in most other countries."

Indian ladies of the aristocracy – both Hindu and Muslim – were secluded in the zenana or *Andarmahal* quarters. They observed purdah, which was considered an essential part of a respectable way of life and also a mark of delicacy and refinement. Hence, there was much curiosity about these ladies and their way of life. The zenana was a world of mystery and intrigue. Some memsahibs who had access to the zenanas provide delightful accounts of these "hoories of the East" and their gorgeous costumes and glittering jewels. We come across a unique mid-18th century account by a "lady of nice observation" published in England in 1743 and reproduced by the American journal *Virginia Gazette*. It is about her meeting with a Nawab's wife in Madras. She describes in details the opulence of the Begum's costume and the exotic richness of her jewellery with several strings of glittering diamonds and pearls.

She adds: "Her person is slim, genteel, middle stature, her complexion tawny, her eyes black as possible, large and fine, and painted at the edges; her lips were coloured red, and between every tooth, which were white and regular, was painted black, to look like ebony ... Her face was done over with frosted work of leaf gold; the nails of her fingers and toes were painted red, so were the insides of her hands; her hair was black as jet, very long and thick, comb'd neatly back and braided; it hung much below her waist." The English woman was "amazed and astounded" by such a picture of luxury and noted that she thought, "she was in a dream sequence all the time."

The classes of women who came into contact with the English sahibs were the bibis or unofficial wives of British officials, the nautch girls and female servants. In the countryside, however, both in the plains and the hills, they saw women young and old out in the open as the rural life was free from purdah. Women could be seen working on farms, drawing water at the wells and bathing at the river ghats. A fine portrayal of Indian maidens by Waterfield in his *Indian Ballads* is reminiscent of descriptions in Sanskrit literature. That seems to have fired the imagination of British artists.

Just as landscape painting was influenced by the British concept of "picturesque," the Western concept of beauty had its impact in the portrayal of Indian women. William Hodges, the first British professional artist to visit India (1780) acknowledged that his portrayal of Indian women was based on ideas of classical beauty.

He was in raptures on seeing village women at the ghats. He watched them bathing, observing that the younger women in particular delayed and lingered, "sporting and playing like Naiads or Syrens." He wrote: "To a painter's mind, the fine antique figures never fail to present themselves when he observes a beautiful female form ascending these steps from the river in wet drapery, which perfectly displays the whole person, and with vases on their heads, carrying water to the temples."

The delightful sight of women at the river ghats inspired many a Company official and soldier to record his impressions in diaries and journals. Lieutenant Thomas Bacon watched women at the ghats of the Ganges. He was captivated by their grace and charm and noted that they could make any Englishwoman envious. He found them "remarkably beautiful, both in feature and figure with faces of a more Grecian mould, their beauty enhanced by the simplicity of their costume and the classical style in which the *chuddur*, or large scarf, was thrown across their figures." He was also "struck by their lovely small feet, and particularly good ankles, and of their free and elastic step as they walked gracefully," beholding an Englishwoman, with her pinching satin shoe and "who, among our starched and tight-laced, though lovely women, would venture to place the charms of her cramped figure in competition with the unshackled graces exhibited among these children of nature?"

Captain Godfrey Charles Mundy, A.D.C. to the Commander-in-Chief, Lord Combermere (1825-30), was romantically inclined towards native women and keenly observed them "laughing and chattering" in the Ganges. He noticed how in the unfrequented

A Bengali lady wearing characteristic jewellery by Fredrick W. A. De Fabeck, c.1860

spots of the river they took a hasty glance up the bank and along the shore, disengaged themselves in an instant from their sari and plunged into the stream. He noted in his journal: "In the ecstasy of the moment, and in their desire to admit the sacred element to immediate and unveiled contact with their persons, the fair pilgrim did not quite sustain their usually modest and decorous management of their drapery in the river bath."

There is another poetic description of bathing women at river ghats in *Excursions in India* by Captain Thomas Skinner who was thrilled by the sight as they "rose from the wave, and stood with their transparent drapery floating about them to comb their long locks – like mermaids in all but their want of mirrors. When their hair is nearly dry they hold their clean robes like a screen round their figures; and shaking the wet one off them, draw the other close and are dressed in a moment."

Bishop Reginald Heber of Calcutta (1823-26), not immune to feminine charms has made many references to pretty young women in his journal *Narrative of a Journey* which contains some fascinating descriptive material about India. Struck by the style of a pretty young countrywoman at a river ghat, he recorded his impression in the following words:

"She went in with her mantle wrapped round her with much decency and even modesty, till the river was breast high, then ducked under water for so long a time that I began to despair of her reappearance. This was at five o' clock in the morning, and she returned again at twelve to undergo the same process, both times walking home in her wet clothes without fear of catching cold. The ancient Greeks had, I am convinced, the same custom, since otherwise the idea of a wet drapery would hardly have occurred to their statuaries or, at least, would not have been so common."

Heber was also greatly attracted by their skin colour and pointed out that "the deep bronze tint was more naturally agreeable to the human eyes than the fair skins of Europe."

The romanticised image of Indian women was vividly captured by contemporary professional and amateur artists as well. Their portrayal of women of different classes is both sensitive and appealing and true to life. They speak about their physical beauty and charm, in spite of their dark complexion, in superlative terms.

Kashmiri women figure in quite a few accounts and are extolled for their charm and beauty. James Forbes, a noted (East India) Company official (1765-84) in his *Oriental Memoirs* describes a noble lady he met at Surat as "one of the greatest beauties he ever beheld." Richard Burton, the famous scholar pays high compliments in colourful language to Sindhi women while Mrs. Marianne Postans, wife of a Company official, eloquently describes the remarkable beauty of Kutch ladies. About Bengali women it is stated that "in figure she stands comparison with the finest races of the world." Nagar women of Gujarat are praised for their grace and charm and particularly their dark eyes "in whose depth glows a spark of passion round which humour and laughter play." Maratha ladies, especially of the aristocracy, are portrayed as singularly charming and credited with intelligence and refined manners.

The sahibs were particularly struck by the grace and charms of the Bombay fisherwoman. She is described as attractive with a trim figure and a smile on her lips. According to one observer, "her dress is striking; the skimpy mantle or sari is slung tight between the legs and over the upper thigh so that every movement of limb and curve of figure shows in bold lines as the fisherwoman carries her basket on her head to the crowded market."

In the South, Nair women were admired for their unique charm. Some others swore by the women of Canara with their lovely dark eyes and soft glossy hair falling down to the knees. It is observed that British reactions to the physical appearance of native women were influenced by their general

Native lady of Amritsar by Van Smith, c.1880

attitude to beauty of womankind and, also by their association with a particular region of the country, and its people.

As traders, the British had little sense of racial superiority and dealt with Indians on equal terms. Many of them had close friendships with Indian nobles and scholars. The Indian social customs and manners were duly accepted and there were no harsh comments on the status of Indian women in society.

However, by the beginning of the 19th century the atmosphere had started changing. From merchants, the British turned into rulers and therefore, developed a growing contempt for those they

Hinda, presumably the favourite wife of the King of Oudh by George Beechey, c. 1830

now ruled over. In the late 19th century we come across some women authors with more objective and unbiased observations on the status and role of Indian women in society. Flora Annie Steel, a famous literary figure of the period analyses the two opposing estimates of Indian womanhood – the one favoured by most

Englishmen and fostered by missionary reports, which represents it as being thoroughly degraded, hopelessly, helplessly deprived and utterly enslaved, the other which asserts that, on the contrary, the ideals of the Indian women are the highest in the world, and that her conduct is an example, her life free and happy. She explains the fundamental difference between the Western and the Eastern ideals of womanhood. After examining the two divergent standpoints, she holds the ideal Eastern woman at a higher pedestal for her self-abnegation and greater moral courage.

Another woman author, Elizabeth Cooper (1915), admires the Indian woman for her innate sense of modesty, her womanliness, her love of home and children and her feminine qualities which to the Western mind may appear as a weakness, but, in fact, constitute her appealing charm. She emphasises that "if the Western woman offers her gifts of modern education and intellectual advancement, her Eastern sister will not be her debtor if she, by example, presents in return more precious charms of obedience, modesty and loyalty which fundamentally are the priceless jewels in the crown of world's womanhood."

Indian Paintings for the Sahibs

By the late 18th century the British had emerged as the dominant power in India. This in turn encouraged young, middle class English young men to join the East India Company as civilians and soldiers. These newcomers were fascinated by the variegated landscape of the country, its magnificent monuments, and the diversity of its people. They wanted to acquire pictures of their new environment but not all of them could afford to buy the works of British artists engaged in portraying the scenic splendours of India and its exotic people.

So, many British residents and travellers began commissioning native artists to produce paintings of their chosen subjects as mementoes and souvenirs for their friends and relatives in England. The British found almost every

Col. James Skinner, Delhi or Hansi by William Melville, c. 1836

aspect of life in India worth sketching. Their favourite subjects, however, were historic monuments with their novel architecture, people of different classes wearing picturesque costumes, festivals and rituals, crafts and occupations, strange modes of transport, and the nautch entertainment to which the Englishmen had got addicted during this period.

On their part, the Indian artists welcomed this opportunity to work for these new British patrons since the traditional patronage of Indian rulers and their courts was rapidly declining. Indian miniature paintings of the Mughal style were already well known in Europe and England. In order to satisfy and cater to the tastes of British clients, native artists modified their techniques and style and at times adopted traditional indigenous elements. They did not receive any formal training from the British as their accomplished skills were more than adequate to meet this new demand. They gave up using guache in favour of European paper and changed the colour pattern, replacing the brilliant hues of miniature paintings with more muted colours like soft blues, greens and sepia which appealed to the British.

Not surprisingly, there was soon an expanding market for the works of Indian artists. There was also a gradual realisation by the British that their favourite Indian subjects could be depicted more accurately by native artists who were familiar with them. These special types of paintings, a product of the British connection, came to be known as the Company Painting. It dominated the art scene in India between 1775 and 1900.

These paintings form a valuable record of the social and cultural scene in India during this period and also of the historical buildings and monuments, many of which have ceased to exist.

The first region to produce the Company Painting was the Madras Presidency, but within a few years, the new style was adopted by artists in different parts of India. However, these artists did manage to preserve typical local features in their paintings. Sometimes, English patrons engaged Indian artists to copy large oil portraits done by British artists. The engravings of Indian scenic splendours drawn by British artists now available in illustrated books also influenced the technique and style of Indian artists in handling similar subjects.

The Rani of the late Rup Singh of Radaur, from Col. James Skinner's album, c. 1820

Delhi, the great Mughal Imperial capital known for its fabulous wealth and splendour, had for centuries attracted foreign travellers, traders, and scholars. The British captured Delhi in 1803 and within a decade or so it turned into a conventional British-administered station and a favourite tourist spot for European visitors. They came to explore the fabled city, its majestic monuments and also the dilapidated ruins of past grandeur. This led to a great demand for the pictures of these historic sites. Artists in Delhi were only too happy and willing to apply their talent for meeting this demand. Of all the Company School painters, those from Delhi were the most skilful and versatile as they had inherited the art through several generations. The works of their forefathers had adorned Mughal courts and created masterpieces of miniature paintings which are now treasured in famous museums and galleries all over the world. They were quick in adopting new modes of expression as and when required, while retaining their passion for meticulous detail. They were also familiar with a wide range of subjects – portraits, natural history, court scenes, historic events, royal processions, and also literary themes.

Delhi artists made splendid colourful drawings of famous landmarks like the Qutab Minar, Red Fort, Jama Masjid, Humayun and Safdarjung mausoleums, and Jantar Mantar. To meet British tastes and requirements, they replaced the traditional medium of guache with water colours and began using imported paper. The choice of colours was also in keeping with British preferences. The edifices were shown in perspective against a plain background. At the same time, Indian characteristics of aesthetics and sensitive realism were duly retained.

By the late 1820s, recognising the steady demand, artists began to standardise their work and stock sets were produced for foreign visitors. In the second half of the century, ivory became the most popular medium. Paintings were made on oval or rectangular sheets of ivory and either sold individually or mounted in boxes or jewellery.

Besides monuments, the British were equally interested in collecting pictures of the Grand Mughal, the emperor without an empire, and his renowned ancestors like Akbar, Jehangir, Shah Jahan and Aurangzeb. Delhi artists produced several different sets of paintings both on ivory and paper to meet this popular demand. as well. These also included the portraits of empresses and royal ladies. The traditional skill of Delhi painters who could catch a striking likeness of actual figures encouraged another genre of painting – the making of portraits as private commissions. The most popular were portrait miniatures on ivory, matching in quality and finish the British miniatures of the period.

A number of British officials in Delhi at this time were flamboyant characters who were fascinated with the Indian way of life. Far away from Imperial Calcutta, they still continued living with their Indian bibis, smoked hookahs and enjoyed the performance of nautch girls in their mansions. This class of sahibs also took an interest in Indian paintings and even retained local artists. Some of them have been identified from their specific paintings and British patrons. They include Lallji, Jivan Ram, Mazhar Ali Khan, Ghulam Murtaze Khan and Latef.

One of the leading patrons of local artists was Sir David Ochterlony, (1758-1825) nicknamed "Loony Akhtar," who lived in Delhi from 1803 to 1825 and was twice Delhi's British Resident. There is a painting in the British Library by a Delhi artist showing him smoking a hookah and watching a nautch in his mansion. He lived magnificently and entertained like a royal prince. He is known to have engaged artist Jivan Ram to make his portrait, which is now with the Victoria Memorial Hall in Calcutta. William Fraser (1784-1835) also belonged to the same class of sahibs with a deep

A group of dancing girls performing beneath a white canopy by a Delhi artist, c. 1830

love of India. He went to Delhi in 1805 as an Assistant to Ochterlony and rose to the rank of Commissioner and Agent to the Governor General. He was captivated by the natives' luxurious style of living, and adopted Indian ways and had more local friends than Europeans. He also had several native wives and sired scores of children, who it is said, followed the respective religions of their mothers.

Fraser was a generous patron of Delhi artists which is evident from the famous *Fraser Album* discovered in 1979 with his family papers in Scotland. Easily this is the finest collection of Company School paintings, with over a hundred water colours depicting a wide range of Indian characters and the patterns of social and cultural life in the city. These paintings are unique both in quality and subject matter. There are portraits of Fraser's staff, his Indian friends and local villagers, which carry inscriptions by Fraser. Noteworthy for their sensitive realism and astonishing detail, the *Album* paintings are of great aesthetic merit as they capture the mood and expression of different situations displaying a lively fusion of Eastern sensitivity and Western objectivity.

The artists who contributed to this *Album* hailed from a guild of the finest Delhi painters of whom only two names are documented – Ghulam Ali Khan and Lallji.

Fraser patronised not only the visual artists but also famous nautch girls of Delhi who were invited to his house for entertainment. There are also a few portraits of these nautch girls in the *Album*. Generous and kind-hearted towards natives of all ranks, Fraser even commissioned a portrait of his peon Umeechund who had once saved his life from an assassination attempt.

Another patron of local artists was Sir Thomas Theophilus Metcalfe who succeeded Fraser as the Agent in Delhi after his murder. He had come to Delhi in 1813 when his brother Charles was Assistant to Ochterlony and lived in Delhi for forty years. He built the famous Metcalfe House on the banks of the Yamuna and had a garden house in the Qutab Minar complex. He commissioned Delhi artist Mazhar Ali Khan to make a large set of paintings of the magnificent monuments in Delhi. Mounted in a family album, the set was entitled *Reminiscences of Imperial Delhi*, with the dedication, "For my very dear girls, 25th November 1844."

Metcalfe's album also contains plans of his two houses and a portrait of the Mughal king Bahadur Shah and various other figures who took part in royal processions. This set, called *Delhi Book* is now well-known through its publication as the *Memories of Lady Clive Bayley* edited by M. M. Kaye under the title *Golden Calm* (1980).

Then we have one of the most striking personalities of the Raj, Colonel James Skinner (1778-1841), famous for his Skinners Horse or the Yellow Boys Irregular Cavalry Corps that took part in many campaigns. The son of a Scottish father and a Rajput mother, Skinner had settled down into an Indian lifestyle with an estate at Hansi, near Delhi, and a large mansion at Kashmiri Gate where he had lavish nautch parties, popular with both Indian and European guests. He took delight in presenting pictures of nautch girls to his guests – the same girls who had been entertaining them. Skinner commissioned several Indian artists to work for him. Ghulam Murtaza Khan was the one to receive a highly complimentary testimonial from him. Another prominent artist who made portraits of Skinner, his friends and other members of his household was Ghulam Ali Khan, noted for portraying a striking likeness of figures, bringing them vividly to life.

Peearee Jan in indoor costume, a dancing woman from Delhi by a Delhi artist, c. 1815 (from the Fraser Album)

James Skinner's famous album, *Tazkiratal-Umara* contains several fascinating portraits of Indian nobles, chiefs of neighbouring states and principalities, and also his friends and other common people engaged in different occupations.

Company Paintings present a fascinating visual record which brings this long dead society back to life. We can learn more from these sketches about the social and cultural scene of the period than from written records in the archives. The Company style did not mark any deviation or decline of the traditional Indian art. It was only a new form in a different mode which in reality retained the elegance, poetic vision, and sensibility inherent in Indian visual arts.

Mildred Archer, a leading British authority on Indian art, considers "Company Paintings as the last original contribution by Indian artists before the modern deluge." The fast-changing modes of visual arts and the advent of the camera led to a sharp decline in British patronage of Indian artists. Company Paintings went out of fashion and by the end of the 19th century this form had vanished from the scene.

An Original Hindoo Painting

KANHYA JEE AND THE GOPIA.

Section III

Fanny Parks – First Indophile Memsahib Traveller, Writer and Artist

Enamoured of India with its picturesque landscape and natural beauty, its diverse people in exotic costumes, its festivals, rituals and rites, its music and dance and even its cuisine, Fanny Parks is one of the most appealing chroniclers of Indian life and lifestyle in the first half of the 19th century.

Fond of wandering and adventure and unmindful of creature comforts, Fanny travelled extensively during her

Lachhmi, the goddess of beauty by Fanny Parks, c. 1840

twenty four-year stay in the country (1822-46) and recorded her experiences in a monumental two volume journal entitled, *Wanderings of a Pilgrim in Search of the Picturesque*. A keen observer with an open mind, she felt at home with native people of different classes and evinced genuine interest in learning their way of life, beliefs, and customs.

She even learnt Persian and Hindi and made extensive use of Hindi words, idioms and phrases in her texts in order to give an oriental flavour to her expressions. Illustrated with sketches and paintings drawn by her, the journal is replete with lively eyewitness accounts of her encounters in India. Full of information on practically every aspect of the Indian social and cultural scene, her journal is a favourite document with historians of the Raj who recognise it as a classic, comparable with the works of famous India experts like Coryat, Roe, Bernier, Tavernier, and Manucci.

Fanny was a great admirer of the picturesque sights offered by India. She enjoyed participating in native festivities at river ghats and temples. She pursued visual beauty with greed, enjoying both "the grandeur of storms" and the hurly burly scenes in towns and villages.

Born in England in 1794, this daughter of Captain William Archer married Charles Parks, an East India Company civilian and came with him to Calcutta in 1822. She was "a woman of boundless energy, both physical and mental, more than usually observant and inquiring, her interest not confined to the home or social life of the English stations. She was full of activity, taking a tremendous lot of exercise on horseback, exploring out of the way places and going on expeditions ... She enjoyed danger, adventure, and solitude, and had no hesitation in setting off alone on long river journeys, for pleasure not necessity, in an unsuitable boat against the stream at the height of the rains or going in a rickety cart into the jungle to look for traces of a tiger."

She was equally impressed by the grandeur of the city of palaces and the luxurious lifestyle of the English civilians and soldiers. She wanted to discover the mysterious India and while travelling in the North from Allahabad where her husband was stationed, she was captivated by the holy cities of Benaras and Mathura and became an eager student of Hindu mythology and iconography.

The grass cutter and the gram grinder by Fanny Parks, c. 1840

She gives graphic descriptions of the celebration of Hindu festivals and ceremonies.

Diwali celebrated on the ghats of Kanpur is made to come alive in her fascinating account (1830): "On reaching the ghat," she says, "I was quite delighted with the beauty of a scene resembling fairyland ... On every temple, on every ghat, and on the steps down to the river's side, thousands of small lamps were placed from the foundation to the highest pinnacle, tracing the architecture in the lines of light. The evening was very dark, and the whole scene was reflected in the Ganges."

She describes how crowds of Hindu worshippers prostrated themselves before the idols of Lord Shiva and Ganesha and then poured Ganges water, rice, oil, and flowers over the images of the gods. She also noted some women sending off little paper boats, each containing a lamp, which floating down the river, added to the beauty of the scene. The river was covered with fleets of these little lamps hurried by the rapid stream. She was so thrilled by the sight that she recorded, "I was greatly pleased: so Eastern, so fairy-like a scene I had not witnessed since my arrival in India; nor could I have imagined that the dreary-looking station of Cawnpore contained so much of beauty."

Fascinated by the legends of Krishna and his *gopis*, she made a study of the popular folklore on the worship of Krishna and Radha and collected an impressive stock of Hindu idols and artefacts which she claimed were far superior to what was held by the British Museum.

Fanny presents herself as a pilgrim to the East and in the introduction to her journal she invokes the Hindu god Ganesha as the source of knowledge and learning and seeks his blessing in her venture. She writes: "O Ganesha thou art a mighty lord! Thy single tusk is beautiful and demands the tribute of praise from the Haji of the East. Thou art the chief of the human race; the destroyer of unclear spirits. The remover of fevers, whether daily or tertian! The pilgrim sounds they praise; let her work be accomplished."

She opens her journal with the well-known Indian proverb, "Let the result be what it may, I have launched my boat." Fanny also acknowledges that she became an ardent observer of Hindu customs and rites and sometimes her friends would tease her by saying, "we expect someday to see you at puja by the river."

Fanny was also enthusiastic about the charpai: "It is the most luxurious couch imaginable, and a person accustomed to the charpai of India will spend many a restless night ere he can sleep with comfort on an English bed." She also became fond of Indian cooking and preferred it to European dishes. She even took a fancy for Indian-made dresses and admired Indian clothes, preferring the flowing lines of drapery to the vile round hats and stiff attire of the European gentlemen, and the equally ugly bonnets and stiff and graceless dresses of the English ladies.

Indeed, in the matter of dress Fanny became a total Indophile. She writes: "In Europe, how rarely – how very rarely does a woman walk gracefully! Bound up in stays, the body is as stiff as a lobster in its shell; that snake-like, undulating movement –

A Barkandaz, a Calcutta policeman by Fanny Parks, c. 1835

the poetry of motion – is lost, destroyed by the stiffness of the waist and hip, which impedes the free movement of the limbs. A lady in European attire gives me the idea of a German manikin; an Asiatic, in her flowing drapery, recalls the status of antiquity. English dresses are very unbecoming, both to Europeans and Asiatics. A Musulmani lady is a horror in an English dress; but an English woman is greatly improved by wearing a native one, the attire itself is so elegant, so feminine, and so graceful."

On a visit to England after seventeen years in India, she could not restrain her indignation at the female fashion of the times: "What can be more ugly than the dress of the English? I have not seen a graceful girl in the Kingdom: girls who would otherwise be graceful are so pinched and lashed up in corsets, they have all and every one the same stiff dollish appearance; and that dollish form and gait is what is considered beautiful!"

Little wonder then that Fanny felt so at home with Indian society that she gives a delightful account of a "dazzling party with nautch girls and musicians she attended at the house of a rich Bengallee baboo (sic)." She also had the opportunity of witnessing the performance of Nickess, then the most celebrated nautch girl of Calcutta whom she describes as the "Catalani of the East." Her fancy for everything Indian led her to learn how to play the sitar. She describes how once some laughing slave girls at an Indian aristocrat's house danced merrily to a tune played by her on the sitar.

Like other Europeans, Fanny was also intrigued by the mysteries of the zenana where ladies of rank were secluded. She was easily the first memsahib to have an access to the zenana where she interacted with the ladies. They seem to have liked her for her warm and sympathetic curiosity and talked to her freely and informally.

Fanny studied the lifestyle and customs of these Indian ladies and even learnt the rules of Indian etiquette. Her intimacy with Colonel Gardener and the women of his family hailing from the Mughal nobility made her acquainted with the inner life of the zenana with all its intrigue, scandal and gossip. Enchanted by the graceful costumes of the ladies, she was particularly struck by the dupatta or the veil and writes: "The *dopatta* is so transparent, it hides not; it merely veils the form adding beauty to the beautiful by its soft cloud-like folds. The jewellery sparkles beneath it and the outline of its drapery is continually changing according to the

A spring bow with poisoned arrow for killing tiger by Fanny Parks, c. 1835

movements of coquetry of the wearer."

Fanny's account of the interaction with the ladies of the Gardener household is both revealing and humorous. She also attended a grand family wedding and gives a detailed description of the elaborate wedding ceremonies and the mighty spectacle of the wedding procession with nautch girls dancing on moving platforms carried by men. She was amazed to find how fortunes were squandered by parents on the weddings of their daughters. Highly unconventional, Fanny had strong feelings about the position of women in society and the denial of education to them.

She also made friends with Baiza Bai, the deposed Maratha queen of Gwalior who impressed her far more than the exotic beauties of the zenana. She wrote, "Her continence is very mild and open; there is freedom and independence in her air that I greatly admire." Fanny supported Baiza Bai's political ambitions and they exchanged views about the universal oppression of women echoing the words of modern feminists. She visited Baiza Bai several times and "liked her better than any native lady I ever met with." She was impressed by the riding skills of Maratha women and found their method of sitting astride far more sensible than sitting on the side saddle. In her enthusiasm, and carried away by her emotions she even wrote at that time, "Were I an Asiatic, I would be a Maharatta."

She gives a fascinating account of Janmasthmi (Lord Krishna's birthday festival) that she witnessed with Baiza Bai and her young princess who was amusing herself on the swing as a necessary part of the ceremony, "after which some sixty or eighty Maharatta women came forward, and performed several dances sacred to the season, singing as they moved on the turf, in a circular dance called the *rasa*, in imitation of the *gopis*; and the *Songs of Govinda*, as addressed by Kaniya to Radha and her companions, were rehearsed at this festival, with a scenic representation of Kaniya and the *gopis*. The listener could not depart after once hearing the sound of the flute, and the tinkling of the *gopis'* feet; nor could the birds stir a wing; while the pupils of the *gopis'* eyes all turned towards Creeshna."

Later, Fanny had the opportunity of calling on one of the Mughal princesses at the Royal Palace in Delhi. She was moved by the pitiable and impoverished state of these descendants of Emperors. So much so, that out of compassion she refused to visit the chambers of Bahadur Shah. She found Delhi, once a magnificent city, just a heap of ruins dotted with the remains of extensive gardens, mosques and pavilions. This desolate sight incited Fanny to quote a couplet of Sadi, the famous Persian poet:

> *The spider has woven his web in the royal palace of the Caesers,*
> *The Owl standeth sentinel on the watch towers of Afrasiab*

The irrepressible Fanny was shocked when she saw some European ladies and gentlemen with the band playing on the marble terrace of the Taj Mahal dancing in front of the tomb. She had admiration not only for the unearthly beauty of this wonderful monument but held it as a sacred edifice. She writes:

> *"I cannot enter the Taj without feelings of deep devotion: the sacredness of the place, the remembrance of the fallen grandeur of the family of the Emperor, and that of Asaf Jah, the father of Arzumund Banoo. The solemn echoes, the dim light, the beautiful architecture, the exquisite finish and delicacy of the whole, the deep devotion with which*

the native prostrate themselves when they make their offering of money and flowers at the tomb, all produce deep and sacred feelings; and I could no more jest or indulge in levity beneath the dome of the Taj, than I could in my prayers."

An extraordinarily high-spirited memsahib, Fanny Parks shunned drawing room gossip, needle work or playing the piano and preferred less lady-like and adventurous pursuits such as shikar, riding, stone-cutting, bird-stuffing, and above all, exploring. She made several trips up and down the Ganges and travelled to remote parts of the country up to the Himalayas. In 1838 she wrote, "How much there is to delight the eye in this bright, this beautiful world, roaming about with a good tent and a good Arab, one might be happy forever in India. I have a pencil instead of a gun and believe it affords me satisfaction equal if not greater than the sportsman derives from his Manton."

Besides giving an absorbing account of

Kaniyajee and the gopis by Fanny Parks, c. 1835

contemporary British official and social life, Fanny's journal also contains over forty full-page illustrations from her own drawings and water colours which display her proficiency in the art. The romanticised or idealised images of people and the views of Indian

A Bengali woman by Fanny Parks, c. 1835

scenes have been vividly captured by her with utmost fidelity and astonishing detail. It is interesting to note that she inscribed her signature on the sketches in the Persian script. In one case she points out that her picture of "Kaniyajee and the Gopees, is based on an original Hindoo painting." It is indeed a superb replica of the original.

Once, she was greatly amused by the story of a native wife telling her husband in rage or jealousy that, "I wish I were married to a grass cutter" because he being so poor could afford only one wife. She sketched her own grass cutter from real life. Then, the graceful demeanour of an ordinary Bengali woman interested her greatly, so much so that she describes in detail her "style of attire – the sari of muslin passed several times around the figure, a remarkably graceful dress." She made a lively sketch of her with all the cosmetics and ornaments adorning her body. This is rated as one of her best sketches, testifying to her talent as an artist.

First published in 1850, Fanny's journal was reprinted in 1975 with an introduction and intensive notes by Esther Chawner who writes that, "In Fanny Parks we have the best of companions to introduce us to all the strangeness and novelty she found in India." It is like a guided tour of the country with all its scenic splendours and panorama of life. She appears to have developed a double loyalty, to India and to England. Her writing is both witty and warm and enriched with an exotic air and colourful detail. It is full of people both European and Indian who come alive with her eyewitness accounts. She presents some rare and revealing glimpses of the days gone by. What she writes is always entertaining and much of it still remains interesting today.

Lola Montez – From Memsahib to Royal Mistress

Lola Montez belongs to that galaxy of renowned coquettes of history, the queens of elegance like Madame de Pompadour, Madame du Barry, Marie Antoinette, and Pauline Bonaparte who shared the glamour and glitter of royalty and enjoyed the power and prestige of the ruling elite. Besides their stunning beauty, grace and charm, these women were also endowed with a fiery intelligence and wit as well as some magical quality which cast a spell on men from all walks of life.

Their mesmerising appeal was attributed as much to their brains as to their bodies. They had mastered the art of captivating men and never doubted their ability to drive away their rivals, if any, in this exciting game of love and passion. The

Lola Montez

daring amorous adventures of Mrs. Thomas James, a very young memsahib of great beauty who created a sensation in Shimla in 1839 makes for fascinating reading when we find her landing in Europe as Lola Montez, a stage dancer, and ending up as the royal mistress of King Ludwig I of Bavaria.

Born in 1818 at Lunmerick in Ireland, the daughter of a British military man, Lola Montez was baptised Maria Dolares Elisa Rosanna, a name pointing to her mother's Spanish origin. She was equally proud of her fiery Spanish temperament and also of her fine British traits, which enabled her to look younger and fresher than other Spanish women. She ran away in 1837 to avoid marrying an old man, Sir Abraham Lumley, and married Captain Thomas James, who was fifteen years older than her and with whom she came to India.

The couple was invited to Shimla to stay with her mother. A remarkably beautiful young woman, Mrs. James became the focus of stares and gossip all over Shimla, the Imperial town known for its rounds of lively parties, romantic escapades, riding, and sports. Those days, Shimla was notorious for its "bright ladies" who outnumbered men and made the place an exciting resort for philandering and frivolity. No wonder, Mrs. James attracted such great attention from all quarters, including the Governor General, whose sister Emily Eden "found her undoubtedly very pretty and such a merry, unaffected girl" and even invited her to spend a day with her at the official camp in Karnal.

Not finding great prospects of name and fame in India, Mrs. James returned to England in 1842 where her husband divorced her for having committed adultery during their journey home. She became a stage dancer and assumed the name Lola Montez. She had little success in England but won some fame in the European capitals of Paris, Berlin, Vienna, and Warsaw. She had utmost faith in her marvellous beauty and her seductive ways of influencing men. For her career as an international adventurer, she found her knowledge of several languages – English, French, and Spanish – extremely valuable and effective.

She always dressed herself with such elegance and skill that every single charm of her body seemed to provoke and attract men. In fact, her sensual beauty and charm and her passionate affairs and scandals were admired and talked about more than her art as a dancer which indeed was nothing above average.

Lola was welcomed and feted everywhere in Europe more due to the legend of her beauty and her rare talent and skill in developing intimacy with the powerful and influential men of every city she visited. Politicians, artists, writers, and poets – whomever she decided to please could not resist her unearthly spell.

"Lola's beauty," says a contemporary writer, "particularly the splendour of her breasts, made men mad every where." A Polish paper published the following eulogy to her beauty when she gave a performance at Warsaw in 1845:

> *"The Spanish poet considers that a lovely woman should have the following twenty-seven beauties – three white: the skin, the teeth, and the hands; three black: the eyes, the lashes, and the brows; three red; the lips, the cheeks, and the nails; three long: the body, the hair, and the hands: three short; the teeth, the ears, and the legs; three large: the breasts, the forehead, and the space between the two eyebrows; three slender: the waist, the hands, and the feet; three plump: the arms, the hips, and the thighs; three thin: the fingers, the hair, and the lips. All those attractions are possessed by Lola in perfect proportions, with the exception of the colour of her eyes – a circumstance which I consider the crown of her other charms. Hair soft as silk, rivalling the shining plumage of a raven falls luxuriantly down her back; on her slender, delicate neck, whose gleaming whiteness puts swansdown to shame, is poised her lovely face. How am I to describe even her teeth? So that the weakness of my pen may not diminish the fullness of truth, I must don borrowed plumes. Marino says of the goddess of love in the 78th stanza of the 8th Canto of Adone: 'On her lovely cheeks sweet flames of roses and rubies glowed, and in her bosom two perfect apples trembled in a milky sea.' Lola's little feet hold the mean between the daintiest Parisienne's and those of a Chinese*

> woman; her lovely delicate calves are like the two lowest steps of a Jacob's ladder leading to heaven;
>
> ... the greatest beauty of Lola, as of all women, her eyes were a deep forget-me-not blue."

Lola was an adventurer non-pareill, a *fillede joir* who is born and not made. Sexual desire played little part in her sport of seducing the high and mighty and climbing the ladder of fame and fortune. She would utilise her sex as a coin to secure adventure and excitement.

Lola had admirers wherever she displayed her seductive charm and beauty. She even captivated the famous composer and piano virtuoso Franz Liszt and accompanied him on many of his concert tours until she got tired of him and parted from him because he ceased to be useful to her. In Paris, she would count among her admirers Theophile Gautier, Alexander Dumas, Janin, Dujarier and other poets and writers. Dujarier was so infatuated with her that he picked up a fight with one of the critics who spoke against Lola and it ended in a duel.

Dujarier was unfortunately killed by his opponent and Lola was compelled to leave Paris. She turned towards Germany where her reputation had already preceded her and she did create a sensation when she arrived in Baden-Baden in 1846. She exhibited not only her physical beauty and graces but also her highly expensive dresses and jewels. Soon enough, she managed to win over King Henry LXXII of Reuss-Lobenstein Ebersdorf. She was excited about having a prince – though of a pocket royalty – as a lover, for hitherto she had succeeded only with bankers, merchants, artists, writers, and poets.

When she went with her lover to his tiny kingdom, her foreign appearance and arrogant bearing shocked the simple folk of the small capital. It was not long before her rough and sadistic actions offended the people of Reuss and the King's officers complained to their monarch. Even the lovelorn prince was shocked at Lola's misconduct, and calling her a "female devil," banished her from his principality. The great adventurer, however, did not get disheartened over this sad episode; it only strengthened her determination to reach higher goals. Her astounding success with the rich and famous revived her confidence, and she managed to extract a fairly large sum from King Henry before her departure for Munich where she was destined to find the man she was looking for.

Every encounter with men of wealth and power enriched her experience of employing the irresistible feminine attraction to her advantage. She explored various ways and means to advance the fabulous art of seduction and pleasing men in the manner they wanted to be pleased. She knew how to bring a man completely under her sway with her voluptuous tenderness, her lively and ready wit, her remarkable high spirits and her instinctive talent of yielding to a man's advances at the most opportune moment. No wonder, she thrived and enjoyed playing with men who were led to believe that in Lola they had finally found a woman who could give them supreme rapturous love.

By the time Lola arrived in Munich in 1848, gossip columns of newspapers in Europe had already carried tales of her beauty, extravagances and discarded lovers, but very little about her success as a dancer on stage. So when she was refused an engagement by the Munich Theatre, she planned to do something spectacular. With absolute confidence in her irresistible beauty and instinctive knowledge of influencing men, she without ceremony marched straight to King Ludwig I whose numerous love affairs were well-known to her. When denied entry at the palace, she raised a hue and cry, which attracted the attention of a senior palace official who got so fascinated by her beauty that he diplomatically persuaded his lord to receive the young dancer.

The sixty-year old King was overwhelmed on seeing her in a closely fitting dress setting off her figure to perfection, particularly the lovely curves of her breasts. Noticing the King's amazement, and his misgivings about whether the beauty of her bosom was actually real, Lola, her vanity hurt by the unsaid suspicions, picked up a pair of scissors and swiftly slit open her dress, exposing the splendour. This bold and passionate gesture totally captivated the King and she rejoiced over her victory with a reassurance that the elderly roué would do everything she wanted. It was not long before the King got her a lovely little palace furnished with the greatest luxury to live in Munich.

He gladly went out of his way to satisfy her every whim and caprice. He was elated with his ageing senses being rejuvenated by the voluptuous beauty of a passionate mistress. This encouraged

Lola to even interfere in the country's politics, to the annoyance of the citizens of Munich. Also her rough and arrogant behaviour agitated the local gentry who were greatly incensed with the King's mistress. She considered herself an autocrat and made costly purchases at Munich shops, like expensive dresses, jewellery and other gifts – all in the account of Le Roi. She signed her letters to business folk and officials as *Maitresse Du Roi*. She was provided with her own box at the theatre next to the royal box in the centre.

King Ludwig was so deeply attached to Lola that he was even inspired to express his feelings in verses such as:

> *Never thou grievest thy lover with heartless and idle caprices;*
> *Never with him dost thou play a wantoning game.*
> *Self-seeking knowest thou not; generous and kind is thy nature;*
> *Bounteous thou art, my Beloved, and ever the same.*
> *Happy is he who commands thy heart for his eager possessing!*
> *Not like those lovers who pine for a mistress unkind.*
> *Thou lovest, and love is for thee a bright and unquenchable beacon;*
> *Constant till death is thy heart, unaltered thy mind.*
> *Hunger and thirst of my soul, unquenched by Italian caresses –*
> *I thought to find happiness so, but found only pain –*
> *"Happiness, happiness," still I cried with insatiable longing,*
> *And such I discovered in thee, thou woman of Spain.*

It was not only the King who was enchanted by the beautiful dancer. She had admirers in Munich both young and old who wore tiepins and carried cigarette cases and tobacco boxes adorned with her pictures. Lola delighted in leading an open life and kept her windows without shutters and curtains so that her ordinary admirers might look into the brightly lighted rooms and observe her existence as a public performance. Her visitors, flirtations, and dressmakers fitting dresses on her naked body were all open to public gaze. Fuchs, a German writer, called her "provocation incarnate" and describes her most aptly in these words:

> *"I am lust,"* said her body. *"My breasts yearn for a lover's caressing hand; my limbs desire to stretch and tighten themselves in unbridled and eternal lust."* Her body sang this song in fascinating rhythm.

Lola employed all her skills to display her sensual beauty to provoke and attract men who found in her the incarnation of the eternal form of passion. She had almost perfected the art of dressing herself in such a fashion as to appear in a man's imagination completely naked; she chose to wear a closely fitting riding costume to exhibit better the undulations of her bosom and inert movements of her thighs thereby producing an effect of nakedness without showing anything. Everything about her provoked desire; her every gesture promised pleasure. She almost succeeded in raising her eroticism to the level of a work of art.

The bourgeois classes of Munich with their noble concepts of morality and decency were horrified with Lola who seemed lust incarnate. At the same time, her arrogant and callous behaviour and utter disrespect for law and justice brought scorn from the people, earning her the title of "devil woman." Despite her great influence over the King, who did everything she wanted, Lola never succeeded in winning a place in aristocratic society. Many luminaries of high society kept their contacts with the royal mistress a secret for the sake of appearances. Eventually, she went too far and there was a lot of hue and cry against the royal favourite, who was held responsible for all the King's faults. To overcome the popular clamour, the King removed his eccentric mistress from the scene and sent her to Weinsberg to a mesmerist for "driving the devil out of her," as she was said to be possessed. Lola did not submit to the "devil cure" and managed to return to Munich, but King Ludwig dismissed her.

Lola went to England in 1849 and got married to George Heald, but was prosecuted for bigamy since her earlier marriage had not been legally dissolved. She escaped with her husband George to Spain where he died in 1853. Later, she went to New York to pursue her career as a stage dancer and married P. P. Hull, a rich American. But she left him, and then in 1859 she met an old friend who influenced her to follow the path of religion. She died in 1861 while engaged in charitable services for fallen women.

From Farzana to Begum Joanna Sumroo

Not much is known of Begum Sumroo's early life except that she hailed from some village near Meerut and in

H. H. Begum Sumroo by Lowes Dickinson, c. 1820

1760 was a member of a nautch girls' troupe in Delhi. Her meteoric rise from the lowly rank of a nautch girl to the high status of Begum at a very young age bears testimony to her shrewdness, diplomacy, mastery in strategy, and iron will in the face of heavy odds.

Begum Sumroo figures in quite a few contemporary journals and writings of East India Company officials and other

European travellers. Her extraordinary personality combining the role of a ruler, warrior, general administrator, and a devout Catholic, and also her fascinating career during the political turmoil of the late 18th century have aroused the interest of historians, scholars, and even fiction writers.

Hence, much has been written about this remarkable woman and there are varying descriptions of the Begum's character and her doings. It was around 1767 that Farzana, a young girl in her teens, caught the fancy of Walter Reinhardt, a German soldier of fortune who bought her from the directress of the nautch troupe and took her into his zenana. Within the limits of the zenana, women were free enough to indulge in their pursuits and many of them even took keen interest in politics, supporting one faction or another to establish their personal prestige and power over their lord and master.

In addition to her beauty, Farzana was endowed with sharp intelligence and she succeeded in winning over the confidence of Reinhardt and thus established her powerful influence over him. So, within a short period of time she graduated from the title of a concubine to that of a wife. In spite of his first wife Bahai Begum, Farzana was formally united to Reinhardt, who through many vicissitudes had achieved a position of eminence as a freelance soldier. He and his brigade of European mercenaries and Indian troops were in considerable demand with the princes of the day.

After her marriage, Farzana assumed the little of Begum Le Sombre or Begum Sumroo. Reinhardt adopted the name Summers which his French comrades changed to Le Sombre and Indians to Sumroo. Another version attributes the nickname Le Sombre to his grim expression and dusky complexion.

After serving different native rulers, Reinhardt joined the services of the Mughal Emperor Shah Alam who put him in charge of the Fort at Agra as General Sombre. While at Agra, Begum Sumroo adopted an Indo-European lifestyle and felt at ease in the company of European men and women. She picked up a smattering of English and French but those were the days when sahibs were conversant with Persian and Urdu. With her sharp intelligence, the Begum learnt a lot during social gatherings about political intrigues, management of troops, and military campaigns.

In 1774 the Emperor granted Reinhardt the principality of

Sardhana, situated in the Doab which extended from Aligarh to Muzaffarnagar, covering a very fertile land producing corn, cotton, and tobacco and bringing an annual revenue of six lakhs of rupees, which was more than enough to maintain his troops with their European officers. Sombre made Sardhana the centre of his administration and built a palace there for his residence. He settled down there for the first time in his life after long years of wandering, to lead the life of a country gentleman. Tired of roaming and in his late fifties, he wanted to enjoy a carefree life with a stable income and a dignified status.

Begum Sumroo encouraged him in this respect by taking over the burden of the administration into her own capable hands, and exercised her husband's powers and authority. The Begum had learnt a great deal from him in matters of statecraft and was well equipped to handle difficult situations arising out of disloyalty or treachery by any of their retinue. She had also mastered the art of self-preservation and furthering of one's own interests at all costs.

This life of ease at Sardhana however did not last long. In 1777 Sombre was appointed military and civil governor of Agra city to support the Mughal drive to complete the subjugation of the Jats and to stabilise Mughal control of Agra.

Sombre died in Agra in 1778, leaving his estates and the principality of Sardhana to his favourite Begum Sumroo. His brigade of troops accepted her as their leader and she in turn was clever enough to pledge her allegiance to the Mughal Emperor, who endorsed her succession and blessed her assumption of charge in Sardhana as its chief. Surrounded by Rohillas, Sikhs and others who coveted the agriculturally rich territory of Sardhana, Begum Sumroo with her disciplined troops bravely crushed their raids and in course of time established her reputation as a competent ruler and a fearless warrior. This in turn induced some Europeans to join her camp. She even won the praise of Mahadji Rao Scindia, the dominant force in North India who provided protection to the Mughal Emperor.

It was in 1787 that the Begum rushed with her troops to Delhi to save Shah Alam from his rebels and in return the Emperor bestowed her with the title "Zeb-un-Nissa" or the Ornament of her sex.

The Begum was impressed by the teachings of some missionaries at Agra who had had their mission there from Akbar's time. She invited them to Sardhana and embraced Christianity. She was baptised at the age of around forty by a Roman Catholic priest and given the name "Joanna" on May 7, 1781. The command of the troops under the Begum devolved successively upon Badurs, Evans, Dudrenee and finally upon Monsieur Le Vassoult, a French gentleman of birth and education who had earlier served with the French army in India under Duplex and later in Scindia's forces.

Another soldier who joined the Begum around the same time was George Thomas, who from a quartermaster on board a ship raised himself to the position of a battalion commander and led several military missions against neighbouring principalities. On one occasion Thomas showed his daring by leading his troops to rescue the Emperor who had been ambushed by another rebel, Najaf Quli Khan, while the Begum sat in her palanquin and watched. She rewarded Thomas by gifting him Maria, one of her very beautiful slave girls and a substantial dowry.

In order to secure his ascendancy against his rival Thomas, Le Vassoult proposed marriage to the Begum and was accepted. As a consequence, George Thomas left her service in 1793. The Begum, however, kept her marriage a secret from her troops and did not change her name.

Le Vassoult kept his distance from other European officers and did not like Begum Sumroo entertaining them at their table. The troops did not like his proximity to the Begum and became rebellious. Faced with these unpleasant situations, Le Vassoult and the Begum decided to quit Sardhana and settle down in some peaceful British territory. He approached the British authorities for safe conduct to Farukkabad where they wished to live in peace, free from the worries and headaches of administering Sardhana which they offered to hand over to the British.

The Begum also addressed a communication to Governor General Sir John Shore seeking British protection. The Governor General gave his consent to the proposal and the couple left Sardhana secretly. In the meantime Sardhana troops stationed on duty at Delhi somehow got intimation of this agreement and under the leadership of Sombre's son from his first wife, they rushed to seize the Begum and her husband. When Le Vassoult heard of their coming, he made a suicide pact with the Begum that they would kill themselves rather than suffer humiliation and torture at the hands of their captors. The Begum got into her palanquin with a dagger in her hand as Vassoult mounted his horse and rode by her side. They had hardly covered three miles from Sardhana when they were overpowered by the troops. Le Vassoult asked the Begum whether she remained firm in her resolve to die with him rather than submit to the indignities that threatened them.

"Yes," she replied, showing him the dagger firmly grasped in her right hand. He drew a pistol and, without a word, shot himself and fell down dead on the ground. The Begum stabbed herself but survived and was taken back to Sardhana and put in prison.

The Begum was not prepared to give up and her strong instinct of self-preservation inspired her to seek help from George Thomas, the one time rival of her dead husband. George marched to Sardhana with his cavalry and challenged the Begum's captors with a declaration that Scindia's force was on its way to join him. The mutineers got frightened and surrendered without any fight. The Begum was reinstated with full honour and decorum. She soon realised that with the changing political scene following the demise of Mahadji Scindia in 1794, and the ascendancy of British power in North India under Lord Wellesley, it would be difficult to continue as an independent ruler. Also the Mughal Emperor had lost all authority and was at the mercy of the East India Company.

The Begum's position became precarious after the British capture of Delhi in 1803. Briefly, she took an anti-British posture by sending an emissary to Ranjit Singh's court in Lahore and to Holkar in Indore, but then she changed her stance and approached her friend Davide Ochterlony, the British Resident of Delhi in February 1804 for British protection. She had always extended lavish hospitality to all British residents in Delhi whom she used to invite to her palace in Sardhana. So, finally with the support of Lord Lake and Ochterlony, a treaty was concluded with her in 1805 whereby in return for placing herself under British protection she was restored the possession of her principality of Sardhana with all the rights and privileges she had enjoyed before. At the same time it was laid down that since she had no children, after her death, Sardhana and her other immovable assets would be acquired by the British authority.

Begum Sumroo, fully secure with ample wealth, honour, and prestige, spent the last thirty years of her life in peace and prosperity supporting the cause of Roman Catholic missionaries. With an annual revenue of nine lakhs, she continued to maintain a large army, more for pomp and show than for any actual need. She was generous towards religious charities and donated one and a half lakh rupees to the See of Rome and also to missionary educational institutions in North India. She also built a magnificent cathedral at Sardhana. Completed in 1822, it was designed by an Italian architect and embellished with decorations brought from Switzerland and France.

Most of the foreign accounts describe Begum Sumroo as a kindhearted, benevolent, and good woman. She had an uncommon wisdom and judgement and a masculine resolution. Though of small stature, her *rooab* (dignity, or power of commanding personal respect) was greater than that of most persons of her days. She had adopted European modes of social intercourse, appearing in public on an elephant, in a carriage, and occasionally on horseback with her hat and veil, and dining at the table with gentlemen. She often entertained Governor Generals and Commanders-in-Chief, with all their retinues, and sat with them and their staff at the table, and for some years kept an open house for the society of Meerut; but in no situation did she lose sight of her dignity.

She retained to the last the grateful affections of the thousands who were supported by her bounty, while she never ceased to inspire the most profound respect in the minds of those who every day approached her, and were on the most unreserved terms of intimacy.

Lord William Bentinck was an excellent judge of character; and the following letter shows how deeply his visit to that part of the country impressed him with a sense of her extensive usefulness:

To her highness the Begum Sumroo

My esteemed Friend, – I cannot leave India without expressing the sincere esteem I entertain for your Highness's character. The benevolence of disposition and extensive charity which had endeared you to thousands, have excited in my mind sentiments of the warmest admiration; and I trust that you may yet be preserved for many years, the solace of the orphan and widow, and the sure resource of your numerous dependants. Tomorrow morning I embark for England; and my prayers and best wishes attend you, and all others who, like you, exert themselves for the benefit of the people of India.

I remain,

With much consideration

Your sincere Friend,
M W Bentinck.

(signed)
Calcutta, March 17, 1835

Begum Sumroo died in 1836 leaving behind more than half a million pounds. She was buried with full honours. A memorial mass was held in Rome on the occasion of her third death anniversary in 1839.

Section IV

Holi and Diwali – Two Queens of Festivals

Holi, the festival of spring, had always been popular in India for its colourful hilarity, fun, and laughter. It had special attraction for the sahibs. The British accounts of Holi describe it as a carnival of the Hindus, a time of universal merriment and joy and a license of all kinds. The ceremonies and sport linked with Holi are compared to those of the Portuguese Christmas. It was an occasion when in their excitement people would forget all distinctions of caste, class, age, sex, and religion.

A holi scene at Calcutta by C. Belnos, c. 1820

An ancient festival celebrated during Vedic times in honour of Kama, the God of love, Holi was an expression of passionate feelings aroused by the spring season and the joy which the revival of nature diffused. Mughal kings took keen interest in the feasts and festivals of the Hindus. Akbar associated Holi with court celebrations and it was the most popular day for rejoicing with music and dance. Colour throwing was a lively part of the festivities. Holi, also called Id-i-Gulabi, marked the commencement of the New Year and both Hindus and Muslims celebrated the event with great zeal amidst hysterical outbursts of joy.

The Nawab of Awadh, like the later Mughal emperors, continued the tradition of Akbar's time of celebrating Hindu festivals in his court. Mir Taqi Mir (1722-1808), one of the greatest Urdu poets, hailed in beautiful verses the celebration of Holi in Awadh in which the Nawabs themselves participated. Holi was also portrayed as a feast in honour of Lord Krishna and his dalliance with the *gopis*. Images of the deity were carried about on elephants, horses, and in palanquins in processions with the multitude singing in praise of Krishna and hailing the arrival of spring.

The sahibs were particularly struck by the extraordinary behaviour of the submissive common people who took liberties with their lords and masters as they got excited with licentious joy during the Holi festivities. Mrs. Postans records in her journal (1838) that "on such occasions of national mirth, the Hindu in his intercourse with the British could cast off his inhibitions and appear in a natural and unaffected character. He gives license to his general disposition, and laughs, sings and adorns himself with garlands, as if he still inherited his native soil, in a happy state of constitutional freedom."

British observers were greatly impressed by the orderliness of these colourful festivities. M. Elphinstone, a scholar-cum-administrator, describes (in the 1820s) the sports in which people eagerly joined in during Holi: "The boys dance round fire, sing licentious and satirical songs and give vent to all sorts of ribaldry against their superiors, by whom it is always taken in good part. The great sport of the occasion, however, consists in sprinkling each other with yellow liquid and throwing a crimson powder over each other's person. The liquid is also squirted through syringes and the powder is sometimes made up in large balls covered with isinglass, which break as soon as they come in contact with the body. All ranks engage in this sport with enthusiasm and get into the spirit of the contest, till all parties are completely drenched

Diwali or Festival of Lamps, Rajpootana by William Sampson, c. 1860

with the red powder that they can scarcely be recognised. A great prime minister will invite a foreign ambassador to play the Holi at his house, and will take his share in the most riotous parts of it with the ardour of a school boy."

According to Bishop Heber (1828), "Holi is an occasion when drunkenness is common among the Hindus." In Gujarat, Forbes mentions in his *Oriental Memories* that a favourite diversion, very much similar to that on April 1 in England, was to "send people on errands and expeditions that are to end in disappointment and raise a laugh at the expense of the person sent."

Holi celebrations in the court of Scindia in Gwalior come alive in a fascinating account (given in 1809) by Thomas Broughton who took part in the festivities there: "When we visited Seendhiya" (sic), he writes, "to partake of this curious amusement, he received us in a tent, erected for the purpose. In front were assembled all the dancing girls in camp. We went dressed for the occasion in white linen jackets and pantaloons. The Maharaja himself began the amusements of the day by sprinkling a little red and yellow water upon us from *goolabadans*, which are small silver vessels kept for the purpose of sprinkling rose water at visitors. Everyone then began to throw about the *abeer* and squirt at his neighbours as he pleased. We were alternately powdered and drenched till the floor on which we sat was covered some inches in depth with a kind of pink and orange coloured mud. Such a scene I never witnessed in my life."

Then Broughton describes the performance of the dancing girls "bedecked with gold and silver lace, their tawdry trappings stained with patches of *abeer*, and dripping, like so many Naiads, with orange-coloured water, now chanting the Holi songs with all the airs of practised libertinism, and now shrinking with effected screams beneath a fresh shower from the Maharaj."

"The Holi songs," he adds, "are not necessarily indelicate. In the following one, Krishna, in his youthful character of *Kanaiha* or the beloved, is described as attacked by a party of *Gopes* or maids, of Mathura during the time of Holi. As it portrays, with much accuracy and spirit, the peculiar customs of that festival, I have translated it:

> *While some his loosen'd turban seize.*
> *And ask for Phag, and laughing teaze;*
> *Others approach with roguish leer,*
> *And softly whisper in his ear.*
> *With many of scoff, and many of taunt,*
> *The Phagoon some fair Gopees chant;*
> *While others, as he bends his way,*
> *Sing at their doors Dhumaree gay.*
> *One boldly strikes a loving slap;*
> *And clouds of crimson dust arise*
> *About the youth with lotus-eyes.*
> *Then all the colour'd water pour.*
> *And whelm him in a saffron shower;*
> *And crowding round him bid him stand,*
> *With wands of flowers in every hand."*

Broughton also describes the celebration of Holi by the ladies who assembled in tents or houses, had nautch parties all night and drenched one another with coloured water. No men, however, were admitted to these select parties except their husbands or sometimes their brothers of a tender age.

A somewhat similar account is given by Miss Fane, daughter of the British Commander-in-Chief, Sir Henry Fane, when he was invited along with his staff to participate in Holi festivities by

Maharaja Ranjit Singh at his palace in Lahore on March 22, 1837. It was a novel experience for her to see the Maharaja and his nobles as well as her father with his staff all appearing as a mass of red and yellow-skin, hair, clothes all begrimed.

Sir John Malcolm in his *Memoir of Central India*, (1823), writes that the Holi festival was most popular with the lower classes. "During the carnival, which lasts four weeks, men forget both their restraints and distinctions. The poorest may cast the red powder upon the head of his lord, the wife is freed from her habitual respect to her husband, and nothing but the song and dance is heard."

Contemporary writings document British attendance and participation in the Holi festivities. In the East India Company's army, the participation of British officers in Holi was a matter of etiquette. For sepoys, the Holi festival was a season of mirth and relaxation. They were delighted to see their European officers joining them in dance and music and playing with them. The sepoys enjoyed introducing their officers' names in their Holi songs and the greater the indecency attributed to each individual, the louder the burst of laughter and applause. It is, however, also mentioned that this festive behaviour in no way affected the general discipline of the army as seen in the following observation:

Celebration of Holi by Mubarak-ud-Daula, Nawab of Murshidabad by an Indian artist after a painting by George Farington, c. 1785

"It is perhaps a peculiar, and certainly a pleasing trait in the Hindoo character, that such licence is never known to produce any real relaxation in the respect for their officers, and obedience to orders, for which the Bengal Sipahees are so justly celebrated: on the contrary, they who can occasionally relax, and join with them in such innocent amusements, are commonly the officers to whom the men are most evidently and warmly attached."

Holi, our great festival of spring marked by its colourful hilarity of fun and laughter, has over the ages continued to hold its pre-eminent place in our festival calendar. Public enthusiasm for it today is as dazzling as it was in the days gone by.

Another festival which held the pride of place and a special attraction for the sahibs was Diwali, the "feast of lamps." Colonel Todd, famous for his early 19th century classic, *Annals of Rajasthan*, traces the origins of this "Grand Oriental Festival" to Central Asia. He writes that the Egyptians who furnished the Grecian pantheon, held these solemn festivals, also called the "Feast of Lamps, in honour of Minerva at Lais and from there it radiated to remote China, the Nile, the Ganges and the shores of the Tigris."

In his account of Diwali, one of the most brilliant fetes of Rajasthan, Colonel Todd states that: "The Feast of Lamps is in honour of Lakshmi, the wife of Vishnu, the goddess of wealth, when every city, village and encampment exhibits a blaze of splendour. The potters' wheels revolve for weeks before the festival, solely for the manufacture of lamps (*diwa*) and from the palace to the peasant's hut, everyone supplies himself with them in proportion to his means, and arranges them according to his fancy.

"Stuffs, pieces of gold, and sweetmeats are carried in trays and consecrated at the temple of Lakshmi. On this day, it is incumbent on every devotee of Lakshmi to try the chance of the dice, and from their success in the Diwali, the prince, the chief, the merchant and the artisan, foretell the state of their coffers for the ensuing year."

We have another account from Tom Moore, the celebrated poet of *Lalla Rookh* that ascribes the "feast of lamps" custom to China where once the daughter of a famous Mandarin, walking one evening on the shore of a lake fell in and was drowned. The afflicted father with his family ran hither and thither to find her and ordered a great number of lanterns to be lighted. All the inhabitants thronged after him with torches.

The following year they made fires upon the shores on the same day. They continued the ceremony every year – everyone lighted his lanterns, and by degrees it grew into a custom which spread to Central Asia.

The Reverend Ward in his *Religion of the Hindoos* (1817) gives but a meagre account of the festival and admits that he cannot trace its origin. "In the month of *Kartik*," he says, "The *Hindoos* suspend lamps in the air on bamboos in honour of the gods and in obedience to the *Shastras* – as the offering of lamps to particular gods is considered as an act of merit, so this offering to all the gods during the auspicious month of *Kartik* is supposed to procure many benefits to the giver."

Diwali on the ghats of Kanpur is brought alive in a fascinating account (1830) by Fanny Parks. "On reaching the ghat," she says, "I was quite delighted with the beauty of a scene resembling a fairyland ... On every temple, on every ghat, and on the steps down to the river's side, thousands of small lamps were placed from the foundation to the highest pinnacle, tracing the architecture in the lines of light. The evening was very dark, and the whole scene was reflected in the Ganges."

It was not uncommon for the sahib's houses to be illuminated on Diwali night. The Godden sisters in their biographical work, *Two Under the Indian Sun*, offer a vivid account of Diwali celebrations in the early part of the 20th century. "We always kept Divali in our home and all day, we helped or hindered Guru, Govind and all other gardeners as they made the lamps ready and set them on the arch verandah railing and window ledge.

"The Muslim servants joined in the excitement for this was a festival enjoyed by everyone; father told us that the Moghul Emperor Akbar had illuminated his palace on this night."

Thrilled with their illuminated house, they would go up to the rooftop to catch a view of the bazar, a ribbon of brightness, and enjoy the sight as the little pointed gold flames flickered and swayed gently, and shone steadily again.

Diwali continues to hold its pre-eminent position as the queen of Indian festivals.

Imperial Lahore - The Paris of the East

Lahore, the gateway to the Indian sub-continent, has a long and ancient past. Situated on the banks of the river Ravi, famous in history as the camping ground of the early Aryans, Lahore was founded according to popular tradition by Lava, one of the twin sons of Rama, king of Ayodhya, the hero of the *Ramayana*.

Inside the Exhibition Hall, Lahore, 1864

The name of this illustrious city also figures in legends and quasi-historic traditions of other Hindu domains associated with the age of chivalry and ancient civilisation. There was something strikingly unusual about this golden land of dreams and legends. For centuries, the city had attracted trade caravans, plundering hordes, and conquerors in search of wealth and power.

No city in the sub-continent can boast of a more stirring or more turbulent history, or a stronger vitality than Lahore, a city ruled by Hindu kings, Mughal emperors, Sikh monarchs, and British sovereigns. Scholars, historians, and travellers passing through Lahore were enchanted by its majesty and grandeur.

In the hey day of its glory as the Imperial capital of the Mughals, a proverbial saying often heard was that "Isfahna and Shiraz together would not equal even half of Lahore." The city was also associated with royal romances. Anarkali's tomb here recalls her tragic love affair with Prince Salim who later ascended the throne as Jehangir. It was in Lahore that Jehangir first saw Mehar-un-Nisa who became the celebrated Empress Noor Jahan. Dara Shikoh was charmed by Ra-no-dil, a dancing girl of Lahore, and married her. Another colourful and dazzling romance was that of Lal Kunwar and the Mughal Emperor Jahandar Shah, the grandson of Aurangzeb.

Lahore finds mention in the eminent English poet Milton's classic, *Paradise Lost.* Thomas Moore in his celebrated work *Lalla Rookh* (1817) describes the glittering life and pageantry among the palaces, domes and gilded minarets of Lahore.

Rudyard Kipling, the Noble Laureate who was raised in Lahore, immortalised the city in his writings.

Following the downfall of the Mughals, Sikhs became masters of the city under Maharaja Ranjit Singh. After his death in 1839, his successors fought with one another and there was anarchy. The British stepped in and annexed Lahore in 1849. As the capital of the British province of Punjab, Lahore regained its old grandeur and dignity. The British Government enforced the rule of law, introduced a modern system of administration and established institutions in order to maintain the Raj. Lahore dominated the whole of the North West and emerged as the fortress of the Indian empire.

By the turn of the 20th century the British Raj had brought in its wake an era of unprecedented peace and prosperity. Punjab, the "sword arm" of Imperial India, was transformed from a poor region into the richest farming area of the country. Consequently, Lahore witnessed great progress in every field – material, social and cultural. By the early thirties, Lahore had regained its splendour, with modern buildings coming up on the Mall and elegant European houses in the Civil Lines area. Many desolate parts of the city were transformed into pleasant gardens, grassy lawns, and metalled roads lined on either side with shady trees. The moat around the walled city was filled up and turned into a beautiful garden, which encircled the old city with its thirteen historic gates.

With its growing prosperity and economic activity, many new residential areas were developed in different parts of the city. The most novel experiment was the construction of a modern township – Model Town – about six miles from the centre, with spacious bungalow-type houses owned by the upper middle classes of all communities.

The new administrative set-up in the Punjab also opened up many employment opportunities in civil services, legal, medical and teaching professions as well as in commerce and industry. With its chain of colleges and professional institutions, Lahore emerged as the leading centre of education in North India. Apart from Government schools and colleges, the missionaries were equally active in setting up their own educational centres in Lahore. This in turn inspired Hindu, Sikh and Muslim organisations to follow suit. The Arya Samaj and the Anjuman Himayat-i-Islam supported by local donors played a significant role in the spread of education among the common people. Other noteworthy contributions in this field were made by renowned Punjabi philanthropists, Sardar Dyal Singh and Sir Ganga Ram.

Punjab University, established in 1882, was the oldest institution of higher learning in India after the three universities in the Presidencies. Lahore had more colleges and schools for both boys and girls than even the Presidency towns of Calcutta, Bombay, and Madras. The famous Government College, opened in 1864, moved to its magnificent Gothic structure in 1877. This building continues to be a prominent landmark of the city. This college was regarded as a premier educational institution of British India. For women, Kinnaird College, established in 1913 by the missionaries,

A view of Kashmiri bazar, Lahore by William Carpenter, 1855

held pride of place in the country. In addition to other professional and technical institutions, a notable one for specialised education was the Oriental College set up in 1870 to promote the study of classical languages – Arabic, Persian and Sanskrit. Dr. A. C. Woolner, a German professor of Sanskrit headed this institution and his statue is the only one that still stands on the Mall in front of Punjab University.

With the introduction of English as the language of administration, its study was made compulsory. It was also the medium of instruction for higher education at the university level.

The British brought Urdu with them from the United Provinces. Hindi in the *devanagri* script came later through the influence of the Arya Samaj. The Punjabi language was more of a spoken dialect and did not figure as a medium of instruction even in schools. In fact, the dominant language of communication among the people was Urdu. But the educated elite chose to converse and communicate in English. It was considered fashionable to do so and displayed one's modern approach and outlook on life. At the same time, those well-versed in Persian, the earlier court language now replaced by English, lost their erstwhile status and were forced to look for livelihoods in plebian pursuits.

In the field of visual arts also Lahore was considered one of the leading centres in the country. The city had a rich tradition of painting and after the establishment of the Mayo School of Arts in the 1870s, local artists were introduced to western painting techniques and themes. Many young artists from far and wide chose to pursue their work in Lahore and by the thirties, a number of them had set up their studios there. The most renowned artist of the time was A. R. Chugtai whose paintings were displayed at the great British Empire Exhibition at Wembley in 1924. Allah Bakhsh was another famous artist and both of them specialised in painting Hindu mythological characters, especially the Hindu deity, Lord Krishna. Other artists of Lahore who blazed new trails in the world of painting were B. C. Sanyal, Amrita Shergill, Roop Kishan and Sobha Singh.

Coming to literary activities, the city was again very much in the limelight. There was a chain of reputed publishing houses bringing out books in all languages. The two English dailies, *The Tribune* and *The Civil & Military Gazette* were the most prestigious newspapers of North India. As regards Urdu publications, Lahore held pride of place not only in respect of newspapers but also with highly acclaimed literary magazines and journals of those days like *Humanvun, Alamqir, Adabi Duniva* and *Adab-i-lateefi*. All these had countrywide circulation and carried contributions from renowned Urdu writers and poets of the time. Sir Mohammad Iqbal, the great poet of the East, ruled over Lahore literary circles like a colossus. His poetry inspired people of all communities. Other noteworthy literary figures of those days were Faiz Ahmad Faiz, Imtiaz Ali Taj, Amrita Pritam, Sahir Ludhianvi, Sadat Hasan Manto,

Rajendra Singh Bedi, Krishan Chandar, K. L. Kapoor, Hafeez Jullundhree, Riaz Qadir, and Oevinder Satyarthi. All of them are still remembered for the mighty contribution made by them to 20th century Urdu literature. Old timers still remember how during the forties a number of these luminaries used to assemble and hold their sessions at the Coffee House on the Mall.

The historic entertainment quarters of Lahore on the borders of the walled city were located in Hira Mandi or The Diamond Market. In its heyday, it was the abode of the accomplished, elegant, educated, and cultured courtesans. They were highly proficient in music, poetry, and dance. Their salons were the seats of culture and youngsters were even sent there to learn gentle manners, etiquette and the art of polite conversation. Artists, writers, poets and the rich went there to enjoy both the music and dance and also the company of these accomplished women. Performing arts had been confined to these families in Hira Mandi for generations and theatrical companies during the twenties provided some openings for the courtesans of Hira Mandi. It was, however, the advent of the talkies in the thirties and later the establishment of a number of film production studios at Lahore that provided a real breakthrough for them to display their talents. Later, many of them rose to become leading film stars. Some others earned name and fame as radio artists. The inmates of some houses in Hira Mandi also carried on the world's oldest profession for a living.

The dawn of the 20th century witnessed a countrywide movement for the revival of traditional classical music and dance and Lahore emerged as one of the leading centres in this field. When renowned musician, Pandit Vishnu Digambar from Maharashtra launched his campaign of setting up institutions for teaching classical music, he chose Lahore for establishing the first one, with the common name, Gandharv Mahavidyalaya in 1901. Again, it was in Lahore in 1925 that the American pioneer of modern dance, Ted Shawn and his talented wife Ruth St. Denis, were struck by the performance of a leading *kathak* dancer, Pandit Hira Lal. A number of highly accomplished musicians and dancers hailing from Lahore won many awards and honours and were invited by princely courts, the chief patrons of performing arts in those days.

The advent of talkies in 1931 brought about a revolution in the entertainment world. A number of new cinema houses appeared on the scene while the older ones of the silent days were renovated and refurbished. A few of them exhibited only English movies and so were patronised by Europeans and the upcoming younger generation keen to learn about the history, culture, and social life of the people who spoke English. This also helped them in the study of spoken English. It was fashionable for college students to talk about latest Hollywood movies and popular actors and actresses of those days.

However, the production of Hindi-Urdu films in the thirties could not keep pace with the increase in the number of cinema houses, with the result that some exhibitors hit upon a novel idea of combining a re-run of old films with a live song-dance performance by an artist from Hira Mandi as an added attraction for the viewers.

Other pastimes and recreations included festivals and fairs, which provided a delightful diversion for people of all communities. Celebrated with pomp and show, these were events of social significance and symbols of a composite culture. Hindus, Muslims, and Sikhs happily participated in one another's religious festivals and celebrations.

In the field of sports too, Lahore did not lag behind. Traditionally, wrestling was a popular sport and there were *akharas* (wrestling arenas) in every part of the city where well known wrestlers imparted training to new entrants and also fought bouts. Wrestling matches or *dangals* were elaborate festive occasions where the dignitaries of the city were invited to grace the occasion. The renowned world wrestling champion Gama Pehlwan hailed from Lahore. He had earned the title of "Rustam-i-Zaman" after defeating the European champion Zbysko in London. In other sports like hockey, cricket, and tennis, players from Lahore earned name and fame in the country and were invariably included in the national teams.

Horse racing, one of the oldest sports associated with English Kings was introduced in India during the Raj. The Lahore race course, following the pattern of Calcutta and Bombay, provided great excitement and entertainment to punters, bookies and jockeys. For some, it was more of a social gathering on Saturday afternoons, a status symbol to be seen among the Lahore gentry, both European and native. One could see ladies most elegantly dressed as if they had come for a fashion parade. The highlight of the racing season was the Punjab Governor's Cup Race, which was attended by the Governor and the officialdom. No punter would ever miss this great event and the bookies' stalls presented a thrilling sight when they opened the bidding and the punters began shouting the names of their favourite horses and their stakes.

There were many interesting and novel sights for visitors seeking to get a feel of this lively city. The chief attractions on the itinerary of every newcomer were the *Ajaib* (Wonder House) or the Museum and the *Chidia Ghar*, the Zoo. Between these two stretched the famous Thandi Sarak or the Mall which could compete in beauty and majesty with any other roadway in the world. On both sides were imposing modern buildings, housing leading shops and stores and motorcar showrooms that catered to the European clientele, the native princely order, and the aristocracy. Some Government edifices like the High Court, General Post Office and the Punjab University buildings were glorious symbols of Indo-British architecture. Prestigious hotels, restaurants and bars were also located here. Some of these even presented delightful cabaret shows for their clients. The new Anglicised generation and college students flocked to these spots of entertainment. In the late thirties, Lorangs, Stiffles and Standard restaurants were the favourite haunts of Lahore's gentry.

At the other end of the Mall stood the stately Government House, the residence of the Punjab Governor, built in the late 19th century. With its vast grassy lawns, walkways, stables, and kennels it was then considered to be the most magnificent Government House in India. On the opposite side of the road were the beautifully laid out Lawrence Gardens with their tall majestic trees, some of them brought from England and rows of colourful, sweet-smelling flowerbeds. The place was a popular meeting point for college students. In the midst of these picturesque surroundings stood Montgomery Hall, housing the Lahore Gymkhana Club with its gaily decorated ball-room, an exclusive meeting place for the sahibs and memsahibs. In another part of the garden was located the Cosmopolitan Club for the westernised native elite. Another unique institution in the neighbourhood was the Aitchison Chiefs' College, with mostly European teachers, for the schooling of princes from native states and sons of Punjab chiefs comprising the landed aristocracy.

The Marble Pavilion in Hazuri Bagh by C. S. Hardinge, Lahore, 1846

Lahore was also a shopper's paradise and its Anarkali Bazar was famous not only in the Punjab but all over the country. Stretching over a distance of about a kilometre, Anarkali dominated the cityscape. As the most fashionable shopping centre, it attracted people from far and wide and even visitors from other provinces, who came to Lahore on a spending spree. For them, Anarkali was a vast storehouse of merchandise, both Indian as well as imported. The famous bazar, with a host of restaurants and bars, was also a place of fun, gaiety and laughter. Anarkali was full of life, charming as a maiden in her youth beckoning one and all to partake of her beautiful gifts.

The post-World War I generation had adopted the western dress complete with neckties and headgear of sola hats in summer and felt caps in winter. College students dominated the world of fashion and those from Government College influenced by their European teachers and Hollywood movies took the lead in setting the trend. The fashion-conscious chose to buy imported British material, readymade shirts and even footwear. It was considered important to keep abreast of the changing modes in order to be counted among the fashionable elite. There were also dandies anxious to attract attention who sported outlandish clothes of unusual colours and cuts. This fashionable class was the trendsetter that provided a market for the new products coming chiefly from England, including powders, creams, hair oils, perfumes, health tonics and even high quality brands of cigarettes and liquor.

The late thirties also witnessed notable changes in the women's world. One would see the budding generation of young girls in stylish attire going to college not only in exclusive buses but also riding bicycles on the main thoroughfares. One also noticed young married couples walking together in the city parks and going to cinema houses which was something rare until the late twenties.

Lahorias loved food not only to gratify the taste of their palates but also to improve their health. They attributed their sturdy physique to the intake of milk products in large quantities. They were least worried about the fat content of their diets. They regarded *ghee* and almonds as the supreme source of energy. Fresh fruits and juices were preferred to other eats and aerated drinks. As a result milk bars and ice-cream parlours also sprang up in the early forties. The people of Lahore followed the Epicurus maxim: eat, drink and be merry for tomorrow we may die.

When it came to the freedom struggle, the young college students of Lahore provided leadership to the movement and were responsible for revolutionary activities against the colonial power. In 1919 Lahore students played an important role in the agitation against the Rowlatt Act and the Jallianwala Bagh massacre at Amritsar. Lala Lajpat Rai of Lahore, the greatest orator of his time became a national leader. In Bhagat Singh, Rajguru, and Sukhdev, Lahore gave the country three great national heroes who sacrificed their lives for their motherland. It was in Lahore that the Indian National Congress held its historic session on the banks of the Ravi when Jawaharlal Nehru declared full independence as its goal. Again, it was in Lahore, at its session held in March 1940 that the Muslim League under the leadership of M. A. Jinnah adopted the momentous resolution to achieve Pakistan.

The prosperity of the Punjab was attributed to the priority and preference it received for Government investments in development schemes, including the vast network of canal irrigation projects. The political scene in the province from the mid-20s until 1946 was dominated by the Unionist Party, supported by the landed classes with their ideology of inter-communal harmony and loyalty to the Raj. The Party stood outside the mainstream of either Indian nationalism or Muslim separatism and its leaders, Muslims, Hindus and Sikhs were respected for their honesty and integrity.

It is relevant to mention here that the interplay of historical forces had made the Muslims of Lahore less fanatic and the Hindus and Sikhs also less orthodox and ritual-conscious than elsewhere in the country. The three communities mixed freely and had cordial and friendly relations, subscribing as they did to a composite Punjabi culture which blossomed from the early years of the 20th century. Muslim influence of centuries had left its impact on the citizens' way of life, customs, and manners and even their individual names. Hindus, Muslims and Sikhs had many common first names, distinguishing themselves only by adding a different suffix such as Ram, Chand, Lal, Nath, Gopal, Ray, and Malby by the Hindus, Ali, Khan, Mahmud, Ahmad, Muhammad, Hasan, and Nabi by the Muslims and just "Singh" by the Sikhs. Some of the current common first names were: Iqbal, Barkat, Aftab, Niamat, Haqumat, Ameer, Faqeer, Khusi, Mukhtar, Mushtaq, and Mehar. They had a common name for the almighty God as well. A Lahoria when invoking God would involuntarily call out "Oh Rabba."

A popular saying on the lips of every Punjabi used to be "*Jine Lahore nahin dekhwa, oh iamian nahin*" (one who has not seen Lahore cannot be said to even have been born). A city is not merely its bazars and buildings. It is its atmosphere, ambience, moods of joy and sorrow, madness and sadness, fun and excitement and above all its people who constitute its soul. Here is an enchanting portrayal of Lahore:

> *Old Lahore was gay and youthful,*
> *moving easily with times,*
> *earning well and spending more,*
> *receiving joy and shunning gloom,*
> *it was a city of scholars and lawyers*
> *and a great high court of justice.*
> *The city of Lahore reveals itself*
> *to the eager longing eyes of youth*
> *its charms of landscape and bazars*
> *from Central Bank to Ravi river,*
> *old historic city and new structures*

> *mingled in vivid spectacles*
> *of colorful buildings,*
> *benign nature,*
> *warm-hearted and vital people*
> *of diverse faiths and traditions,*
> *united in confident resolve*
> *to enjoy life and reach its peaks.*
> (Dr. Prem Kirpal)

The Lahorias were so deeply attached to the city and its way of life that they were rarely tempted to seek fortunes elsewhere in the country. So much so that the educated young men looking for employment were most reluctant to leave the city and rejected offers of jobs in other provincial towns. They preferred to hang on in Lahore and wait for suitable openings there.

No wonder Lahore, the most talked about city in the sub-continent and famous for its glamour, gaiety and gusto got the appellation, "The Paris of the East."

Pageantry of Princely India – A French View

European travellers started coming to India in the 17th century when the Imperial Mughal power was at its zenith. Notable French travellers like Francois Bernier, J. B. Tavernier and Jean de Thevanot were perceptive observers of the Indian scene and have left behind fascinating accounts of their experiences.

They were followed in the 18th century by eminent missionary, Abbe J. A. Dubors, who spent nearly thirty years in South India and produced a classic volume called *Hindu Manners, Customs and Ceremonies* which contains a mine of information. This became a reference book for Europeans interested in learning about Indian society.

The most outstanding and detailed account of travels in India is undoubtedly by the extraordinary Frenchman, Louis Rousselet, who spent nearly six years in India (1863-69) travelling extensively all over the country, using all modes of transport, including the newly introduced railways. Rousselet presents an interesting study of India, it's historic monuments, religious beliefs, old civilisation, and the customs and manners of its diverse people. Not connected in any way with the British Imperial authorities, he brought a fresh mind and independent ideas to bear upon his account, free from any preconceived bias or prejudice. He recorded his impressions based solely on his personal experiences. No wonder, he was full of enthusiastic admiration for what he saw.

Not much interested in the India of railways, hotels, and telegraphs, his main objective was to visit the princely states and see for himself the traditional modes of life, the social and cultural milieu and the glamour and grandeur of the courts of native rulers.

The title of his prolific travelogue, *India And Its Native Princes* indicates the chief object of the author. A voluminous book of over five hundred pages, it contains three hundred excellent illustrations which embellish the descriptive text. Rousselet visited the kingdoms of Central India and Rajasthan, which included Baroda, Gwalior, Udaipur, Alwar, Bhopal and some other smaller states. He has given vivid descriptions of the lifestyles of the rulers, their heroic traditions and the romantic history and achievements of their ancestors.

Rousselet was a witness to a variety of entertainment at the princely courts as he enjoyed the lavish hospitality of the magnanimous rulers and nobles. He was particularly captivated by the graceful Indian dances and gives graphic descriptions of the performances, the glittering costumes of the dancing girls, their slow and graceful movements combined with the sounds of a variety of musical instruments. In Baroda, when received by the Gaekwar (sic) in his palace, Rousselet was struck by the sight of several young and pretty dancing girls, "covered with trinkets and attired in their chemises" who had perfect liberty to go anywhere in the palace. "They were even allowed access to the King's apartments where they would seat themselves on the floor and converse boldly with persons of the very highest rank."

He gives a vivid account of the evening scene when the palace was illuminated and "these charming *nautchinis*, with their songs and dances, created a festive and joyful atmosphere while the King and his ministers held court and discussed state affairs." He was also shown a special review of a composing force of troops dressed and armed liked the sepoys in the English service and commanded by European officers. Rousselet was impressed by the disciplined presentation of arms by each regiment as the bands played *God save the Queen*. Another spectacle, which fascinated him was the *savari* (royal procession) of the Gaekwar. He was amazed to see the multitude of people who had lined the streets of the city to see it, and he wrote: "The air resounds with a confused uproar of cries, songs, and music, compared to which the noise of a Parisian fete would be silence itself.

"The procession consisted of regular troops, royal standards bearers, various regiments, followed by nobles and high functionaries of the realm, each mounted on a fine elephant bedecked with gold fringed velvet hung down to the ground." The Maharaja then appeared seated on his elephant on a massive *hodah* (seat) of gold, which was sparkling with jewels. Rousselet wrote that he had never witnessed "even in Europe, a scene of greater pomp, splendour, and solemnity. When the procession had passed I remained completely dazzled by what I had seen. I could not have believed that there still, even in our days, existed a spot where could be found, in all their magnificence, the most imposing pageants of the Thousand and one Nights."

Rousselet was also stunned to see the dazzling collection of crown jewels comprising the most beautiful precious stones, streams of diamonds necklaces, rings, bracelets, and costumes embedded with pearls and diamonds. Conspicuous among these jewels was a necklace in which sparkled the famous "Star of the South," the "Star of Dresden" and other diamonds of remarkable size – probably the most expensive necklace in the world.

At Oudeypore (sic), Rousselet was witness to the celebrations of the Holi festival, which marks the arrival of spring. He was amazed to see how the King and the nobles threw off all restraint and gave themselves up to mirth and revelry. The dancing girls enjoyed unbounded liberty and performed special dances for the occasion, when all propriety was forgotten, and the couplets which they recited during the dance were most unseemly and always alluded to the people present. He saw another dance performance at the royal banquet held at *Khoosh Mahal* (Palace of Pleasure) by the Rana as no entertainment was complete without the dancing girls. Here, the jovial atmosphere with a liberal flow of wine encouraged them to boldly take part in conversation with their superiors and intersperse their dance with pleasantry, which was much relished by the guests. There is also a mention of a bevy of young and pretty nautch girls of the court being sent by the Rana to the camp of Rousselet and his party in order to amuse them with their songs and dancing and lull them to sleep.

Rousselet was also invited to join the royal hunt on an auspicious date determined by court astrologers called *Ahaerea*, or *Mahurat-ka-Shikar*, that is declaration of war against the wild boar. After the shikar, the Rana went to the temple to worship Surya, the Sun god, an ancestor who was held in special honour in Oudeypore (sic). The King's palace was named Surya Mahal and he gave his *darshan* (appearance) to the people from the top of Surya Gokra, or the "balcony of the sun."

The closing of the Holi season festivities was marked by a grand durbar held on the terrace of the palace, in front of the zenana, and was attended by all the nobility of Mewar and a picturesque crowd of courtiers in gay costumes surrounded by elephants with gold and silver trappings. The climax of the function was the arrival of the Rana, resplendent with jewels and diamonds, accompanied by the English political agent. The grandeur and glitter of the gathering dressed in their richest apparel, costly brocades, hereditary jewels and weapons studded with pearls and gems of priceless value presented a memorable experience, which Rousselet recounts in his book with great fervour.

The court of Gwalior did not offer the same attractions as Baroda and Oudeypore (sic) as there was little pomp and display. Politics and the reorganisation of his country occupied the time and thoughts of the prince far more than hunting and festivities. He lived with comparative simplicity but was known for his admirable skills in horsemanship as noticed by the French traveller: "Mounted on a magnificent stallion of Iman, he went through all the evolutions of the high school of India. This royal tilt presented a striking scene. The King, perfectly at his ease, managed his steed with all the ardour and spirit of the Mahratta; the animal reared, plunged, started off precipitately, stopped short, pranced and jumped at his master's will. Horse and rider were equipped with equal magnificence, the rich silken stuffs sparkling with a profusion of gold, precious stones, and feathers; and the pages and attendants in the royal livery, standing in picturesque groups at the extremities of the arena, completed the picture. The last dextrous feat was greeted with a general 'Wah Maharaja!' and the prince dismounted."

There is a description of the ceremony of *utterpan*, marking the close of the durbar. Each one present received a muslin handkerchief, which he placed on the palm of his right hand; the Maharaja then rose and, going up to each European in turn, poured some attar of roses on his handkerchief, and presented him with betel leaves, areca nuts, and cardamoms, at the same time throwing a garland of jasmine around his neck. One of the ministers went through the same ceremonies with the natives. The Europeans then passed one by one before the throne, and, shaking hands with the King and his heir, left the apartments escorted by the court officials.

The only novelty, which struck him, was their custom of having nautch girls at one end of the audience chamber who sang incessantly during the durbar. He noted, however, that the presence of these charming girls with their fine and brilliant costumes did enliven the monotonous ceremonies.

Rousselet had an amusing experience as a royal guest at Ulwur (sic) when for the first time he was chosen as a patron instead of being a customary noble of the court for the religious dances of the *navratri* (nine nights). The troupes of musicians and nautch girls set up camps in the palace garden. "The dance of the *navratri*," he wrote, "was held on the upper terrace of the palace, where an immense carpet covered the ground and torches dipped in resin blazed on all sides, vying with the stars in brilliancy. The huge platform was occupied by a compact circle of women, sparkling with precious stones and spangles, in the centre of which a nautch girl danced with a languishing air to the ancient music of the Indian religion. The scene was really quite romantic. The crowd of women only partially visible by the uncertain light of the torches above us; the star-bespangled vault of heaven; below us the waving tops of the palm-trees and nims diffusing their intoxicating fragrance; the fresh mountain breeze, which came charged with the scents of the forests, all combined to give a peculiar charm to these evenings."

Rousselet was dazzled by another spectacle of a nautch by

torchlight hosted by the Rajah of Punnah when he wrote that "it was truly a scenery befitting these dances with their antique rhythms, and their bronzed dancers glittering with gems."

Rousselet has also given an eyewitness account of the grand durbar held at Agra in November 1866, which was for the first time presided over by a representative of the Queen of England "now seated as Empress of India on the throne of Akbar and Shah Jahan." Among those who attended the assembly were the Maharajas of Gwalior, Jaipur, Jodhpur, and Udaipur; the Begum of Bhopal; the Rajas of Kota, Kishengarh, Bharatpur and various jagirdars and zamindars some of whom possessed very large estates. Rousselet gives a detailed description of the ceremonies of *nazars* (gifts to a superior) offered by the Indian princes to the Viceroy, Sir John Lawrance, and *khillats* (presentation by the suzerain of a title or a present to a feudatory) conferred by the Viceroy.

The Maharajas offered lavish entertainment on this occasion, and there is a graphic account of "a fairy-like entertainment given by the Maharaja Scindia (of Gwalior), one of the most powerful princes of India."

"The Maharaja had conceived the idea of giving an entertainment at the Taj, which the Agra Municipality had placed at his disposal. From the high flight of steps the garden appeared like a gigantean fairy scene, the fountains throwing up showers of glittering spray, the trees covered with fruit and flowers, and the air filled with enchanting music from the orchestras. The long avenues paved with marble presented a dazzling appearance. There were Maharajas and rajahs sparkling with diamonds, governors, diplomatists, and officers covered with embroidery, Indian ministers and Rajput chiefs, and the great ladies of the Court of Calcutta presenting a spectacle of which no European ceremony can give an idea.

"The Europeans were soon seated at the table; the corks flew in all directions, and mirth and merriment had free course; while the Indians remained standing, spectators of the feast without taking part in it. To say how much champagne was drunk that night would be difficult; but more than one British warrior succumbed to the potent influence of the French wine. The cost of this entertainment to Scindia amounted, it was said, to twenty thousand rupees! After supper there was a display of fireworks on the banks of the Jumna. This river bathes the base of the Taj, describing a graceful curve round that monument; and numerous rockets of every description, but all very ordinary, were reflected for an instant in the sheet of water. Scarcely was all again enveloped in darkness when a line of fire was seen floating down the Jumna, lighting up the whole river. This effect was produced by innumerable little lamps, thrown from the bridge of Toundlah into the river, which we watched for some time from the terrace, as they gradually receded with the river into the obscurity of night. At midnight we were entertained with a brilliant concert from the English orchestras, and then the crowd gradually dispersed."

Rousselet's visit to Bhopal was full of surprises, he was astonished to witness the royal bearing of Her Highness the Begum Secunder who had became the ruler after defying the purdah and presenting herself to the people with uncovered face, dressed in the costume of the princes and proudly seated on her horse, the lone woman ruler of a princely state. He describes her as "a woman of about fifty years of age. Her thin face, lighted up by a pair of intelligent eyes, expresses such a singular amount of energy that one must be aware of it beforehand in order to realise the fact that a woman is before you. The costume itself aids the illusion; tight-fitting pantaloons, an embroidered jacket, and a poniard at the belt, have, as a whole anything but a feminine appearance. Her gestures and manners still less remained one of her sex; on the contrary, they reveal the sovereign and the autocrat accustomed to find everything yield to his all-powerful will; but I must add at once that this majestic haughtiness lasted for only a few moments, and soon gave way to a gracious and winning affability."

He was surprised to learn about a Christian princess in Bhopal who bore the name of Bourbon and was held in high esteem. She traced her lineage to a Frenchman, Jean de Bourbon, who had charmed the Mughal Emperor Akbar with his graceful manners and intelligence and secured a high rank in the King's army. Loaded with honours and riches, Prince Bourbon died in Agra but his descendants were awarded estates and official ranks. Finally, in 1816, after vicissitudes of fortune for over more than a century, one of the Bourbon clan, Baltazar, surnamed Shahzahad Mussuah, or the Christian prince, became First Minister of Bhopal State in 1816, and two years later, the accidental death of the sovereign gave him the regency of the kingdom. Faced with a threat from the

Marathas, he cleverly struck an alliance with the English and within a few years, was able to establish an efficient administration resulting in a remarkable degree of prosperity for the people.

Baltazar died in 1830 bequeathing all his titles and rights to his widow Elizabeth de Bourbon, surnamed Doolan Sircar, and to his nephew, Bonaventure Bourbon. By the 1860s – at the time of Rousselet's visit – the descendants of Jean de Bourbon formed a clan of about four hundred families, three hundred of which settled in the kingdom of Bhopal, and acknowledged Madame Elizabeth as their suzerain who held the first palace in the state after the Begum.

Rousselet also saw two extraordinary types of dances in Bhopal – one was by *cathaks*, or male dancers who were fine tall young men attired in very rich costumes who performed the same dances as the nautch girls with great agility and much grace. He concluded that it was as natural for the Begum wishing to raise the social level of women in her kingdom to organise a masculine nautch as for the other rajahs to have a feminine nautch. Another dance, which he found infinitely more graceful and interesting was the egg-dance. The dancing girl carried on her head a wicker wheel round which threads were attached, provided at their extremities with a slip knot, kept open by means of a glass bead. The dancer began whirling around to the rhythm of music and at each turn placed an egg in a loop until the eggs formed a horizontal halo. She repeated the process and without breaking them withdrew each one of them as she continued dancing. Then the dancer stopped abruptly and presented the audience with the eggs contained in the basket. These were finally broken into a plate to prove that it was no trick but a skilful dance form in tune with the music and its rhythm.

The grand monuments of India too enthralled Rousselet as architectural wonders. He was overwhelmed by the magnificence of the Ajanta caves and gives a fascinating description of the temples at Alwar and the royal necropolis at Gwalior. He was struck by the Gwalior mausoleums constructed on the plans of Hindu temples, with a sanctuary surrounded by a graceful pavilion crowned by a dome with a thousand pinnacles of great beauty above which rose a lofty spire.

First Imperial Durbar in Delhi (1877)

The Imperial Durbar in Delhi: The Clock Tower

The 19th century is called the British century as it witnessed the emergence of the vast British Empire and its international supremacy in the political and economic affairs of nations. The Empire was glorified with an ideology defined by the high Victorian concept of fair play and justice. This had an appeal for the British people who would not support an institution that was unfair and contrary to their national code. They were inspired by the sublime importance of the Imperial idea as they were convinced it was benign and benevolent. The global Imperial structure was bound together by the British crown.

In 1876, Queen Victoria was proclaimed as the Empress of India, *Kaiser-i-Hind*. Lord Lytton, the Viceroy decided to use this occasion to hold a grand Imperial Durbar on an unprecedented scale. It was in keeping with the old Indian tradition of having a dazzling and gorgeous celebration or durbar on the occasion of the coronation of a new ruler to mark his sovereignty over his subjects. The durbar was an Indian institution adopted by the East India Company in the late 18th century to display its imperial might and power to native rulers and the people.

By 1800, holding a durbar had become a regular practice with the Governor General at Calcutta where the Maharajas and Nawabs were ceremoniously received. The British emulated the Mughal style and adopted the trappings of Indian royalty as they realised that the exercise of power and authority should be associated with outward magnificence and gorgeous symbols. The public display of Imperial grandeur through durbars became a glittering ritual of the Raj.

Although it was only in 1911 that the Government decided to transfer the capital from Calcutta to Delhi, the historical importance of Delhi was keenly felt after the mutiny and the removal of the Mughal Emperor to Burma. No wonder, Lord Lytton decided to hold the spectacular durbar in Delhi to proclaim Queen Victoria as *Kaiser-i-Hind*. As a representative of the Queen, the Viceroy lived and moved like royalty distributing royal honours from time to time. After much planning, Lytton selected a site just outside the Mughal capital of Delhi for his memorable extravaganza scheduled for the New Year's day of 1877.

The Viceroy was determined to revive Mughal traditions in the grand manner to show the majesty, power, and prestige of the Raj. During the closing weeks of 1876, more than four hundred Indian Princes and their retinues assembled in Delhi. While the preparations were in full progress, the Viceroy arrived on December 23 by train from Calcutta and was received at the station by Government officials and many native Princes to whom he said on alighting:

> *"Princes, Chiefs, and Nobles, It is with feelings of unusual pleasure I find you here assembled from all parts of India to take part in a ceremonial which I trust will be the means of drawing still closer the bonds of union between the Government of Her Majesty and the great allies and feudatories of the*

The Viceregal Howdah

> Empire. I thank you for the cordiality with which you have responded to my invitation, and trust the close of our proceedings will confirm the auspicious character of their commencement. Accept my hearty welcome to Delhi!"

The Viceroy and his family seated on elephants were then taken in procession through the city to the royal tent which he entered amid the blare of trumpets and the thunder of royal salutes from many batteries waking the thousand echoes of the walls and forts of Delhi.

During the whole week prior to the great durbar, Lord Lytton received visits from the Maharajas, the Consuls General, and Consuls of foreign European powers together with a large number of minor chiefs and rajahs. The following report on the great Delhi Durbar was carried by the *Illustrated London News* of January 6, 1877:

> "Each Prince or chief got a commemorative medal – gold for greater princes, silver for those of inferior rank. The Viceroy himself hung it round each chief's

> neck, while the Foreign Secretary made a short speech in Hindustani to the effect that this was a personal gift from her Majesty in honour of her assumption of the Imperial title. The medal, which is large and handsome, bears on one side the Queen's head, and on the other words 'Kaiser-i-Hind' in Arabic and Sanscrit characters. Each of the greater chiefs also received a heavy and beautifully worked banner, emblazoned with the arms of his House, and carried on a gilt pole, which bore the inscription, 'From Victoria, Empress of India. 1st January, 1877.' Two stalwart highlanders supported the banner before the throne: and the Viceroy, rising and grasping the pole, addressed to his visitor some such words as these – 'let it remind you of the relations between your Princely House and the Paramount Power.'"

The culminating scene of the Grand Durbar on January 1, 1877 was one of great splendour. The Governors, the Lieutenant Governors, State officials, and sixty-three ruling chiefs attended

General Bird's-Eye view of the Imperial Durbar in Delhi

by their suits and standard-bearers, with magnificent memorial banners, were grouped in a semicircle in front of the throne. Behind them the vast amphitheatre was filled with foreign embassies, and the native nobility and gentry who had received invitations; and further in the rear was the vast concourse of spectators who had assembled to witness the ceremony. The whole presented a scene of unprecedented brilliance. To the south of the dais fifteen thousand troops were drawn up under arms, including contingents from the Madras and Bombay armies, and the Punjab frontier force. To the north were ranged the minor chiefs, with their troops and retinues. The Viceroy arrived at the camp at about half-past twelve, and at once ascended the throne. His Excellency's arrival was heralded by flourishes of trumpets and a fanfare from the massed bands of the various regiments present. A grand march was played, followed by the National Anthem.

Major Barnes, the chief herald, then read the Proclamation. This part of the ceremony was preceded and followed by flourishes of trumpets, and the Imperial standard was then hoisted. The Proclamation was followed by a salute of one hundred and one salvos of artillery of six guns each, and a *feu de joie* from the troops, the bands playing the National Anthem.

The Viceroy then addressed the assemblage. He referred to the promises contained in the Queen's Proclamation of November 1858, and fully confirmed them. The Princes and the people had found full security under her Majesty's rule. The Viceroy proceeded to explain the reasons for the assumption of the title of Empress, which was intended to be, to the Princes and people of India, a symbol of the union of their interests and claim upon their loyal allegiance, with the Imperial power giving them a guarantee of impartial protection. The Viceroy then severally addressed the civil and military services, and the officers and soldiers of the army and volunteers, conveying to them her Majesty's cordial sentiments of esteem and honour. He announced also that her Majesty, with the object of noting public services and private worth, had sanctioned an increase in the number of members of the Order of the Star of India in British India, and had instituted a new order entitled the Order of the Indian Empire.

Addressing the Princes and chiefs, the Viceroy bid them welcome, and said he regarded their presence as evidence of their attachment

The Imperial Assembly of India in Delhi: The Vice-Regal Procession passing the Clock-Tower and Delhi Institute, in Chandnee Chowk

to the Imperial rule. His Excellency, proceeding to address the natives generally, recognised their claim to participate largely in the administration of the country, and counselled the adoption of the only system of education that would enable them to comprehend and practice the principles of the Queen's Government. Referring to the possibility of an invasion, the Viceroy said that no enemy could attack the Empire in India without assailing the whole Empire, and pointed out that the fidelity of her Majesty's allies provided ample power to repel and punish assailants. The Viceroy concluded by reading the following telegraphic message from the Queen:

> "We, Victoria, by the grace of God, of the United Kingdom, Queen, Empress of India, send through our Viceroy to all our officers, civil and military, and to all Princes, chiefs, and people now at Delhi assembled, our Royal and Imperial greeting, and assure them of the deep interest and earnest affection with which we regard the people of our Indian Empire. We have witnessed with heartfelt

satisfaction the reception which they have accorded to our beloved son, and have been touched by the evidence of their loyalty and attachment to our house and throne. We trust that the present occasion may tend to unite in bonds of yet closer affection ourselves and our subjects, that, from the highest to the humblest, all may feel that, under our rule, the great principles of liberty, equity, and justice are secured to them, and that to promote their happiness, to add to their prosperity, and advance their welfare, are the ever present aims and objects of our Empire."

The address was received with general and prolonged cheering, and after three cheers from the troops, the Viceroy declared the assemblage dissolved. The ceremony of the Proclamation was performed with all pomp of heraldry by the chief herald, Major Barnes, and his assistants. The whole assemblage was encircled by an unbroken line of elephants with gorgeous trappings, and the vast masses of spectators. The weather was splendid. Most of the camps, in addition to their other decorations, displayed the Danish colours, in honour of the Princess of Wales.

After the great ceremony in Delhi on Monday, Maharaja Scindia and the native chiefs sent a telegraphic message to the Queen congratulating her on the assumption of the title of Empress of India. It is stated that on the occasion of the Proclamation of the new title fifteen thousand, nine hundred and eighty-eight good-conduct prisoners were liberated.

The Viceroy gave a state banquet in the evening to the Governors, Lieutenant Governors, and high officials. At the reception in the drawing room tent many chiefs were present, glittering with clothes of gold and jewels. The uniforms of every kind, the dresses of the ladies, the pearls and diamonds of the princess made up a wonderful blaze of colour and flash.

One of the brightest features of the celebration was a release of prisoners again in keeping with an established Indian tradition of royal festivities. Including convicts in the Andaman Isles, about sixteen thousand prisoners were set free. Nor were the poor forgotten, for the new Empress rupee was lavishly distributed among them in Delhi. At night Delhi was brilliantly illuminated and large crowds of people assembled on the plain between the Fort and the Jama Masjid to witness the fireworks, which in splendour were said to surpass anything of the kind ever seen before in India.

On the whole, the first Imperial durbar at Delhi was well-organised in a very dignified and impressive fashion. It succeeded in binding the Indian Princes who ruled one third of India more closely to the British Crown, the ceremonial centre of the British Empire.

Section V

When Predictions Came True: The Brahmin Who Saw Tomorrow

From time immemorial, astrology has wielded either a pervasive or a peripheral influence in many civilisations, both ancient and modern. As a story goes, the renowned Nobel Laureate Sir C. V. Raman was once performing religious rituals with offerings of food to his ancestors in Gaya when someone said to him, "Sir, you are such a great scientist but how can you believe that this food would reach your ancestors?" Sir Raman smiled and replied, "I cannot prove that this will not reach them."

The pursuit of knowledge demands banishment of preconceived notions and prejudices. The universe is

A brahmin priest by Charles Gold, c. 1790

full of mysteries and faith in the supernatural teaches man that he knows much less than he thinks. We should have an open mind on all questions and also keep alive our spirit of inquiry. Recently there have been attempts in the west to re-establish a sound theoretical basis for astrology but without any conclusive results. However, there is no doubt about the popularity of astrology all over the world. It is estimated that more than half the population either believes in it or is interested enough to consult astrologers and read predictions published in the media.

In India, the Vedic period witnessed a remarkable flowering of astrology. There is a vast amount of Sanskrit literature on the subject explaining the complex system and techniques evolved over centuries by learned sages and philosophers. Greek astrology was also transmitted to India through some Sanskrit translations in the 2nd and 3rd century AD. But the techniques of Indian astrology were related to divine revelations and the Hindu doctrine of the transmigration of souls. The role of karma, the Indian theory of five elements (earth, water, air, fire, and space) and the Hindu system of values were also incorporated into the study of astrology.

The second half of the 18th century saw the flowering of British interest in India's history, literature, and civilisation. That was the time when Sir William Jones established the Asiatic Society and scholars like Colebrook and Wilson translated Sanskrit classics and James Forbes produced his monumental *Oriental Memoirs* (1813). An eminent Company official who spent nearly twenty years in India (1765-84), Forbes wrote about his encounter with a brahmin astrologer who startled him with his amazing prophesies.

Forbes speaks about some brahmins who, like the magicians of Egypt and the astrologers of Chaldea, were supposed to "have within them the spirit of the holy gods, and light and understanding, and wisdom in showing hard sentences and dissolving of doubts." Different from the common soothsayers and astrologers found everywhere in India, this special class of brahmins was gifted with a talent marked by deep learning. Forbes met one of this class who was well-known to his circle of friends and colleagues. He relates three episodes in confirmation of the penetrating vision of this brahmin whose predictions came true.

The first one relates to the appointment of the Governor of Bombay in place of Mr. Crommelin who was under orders of transfer back home in January 1767. When Forbes arrived there in 1766 he learnt that Mr. Spencer, the second in Council had been appointed Crommelin's successor in the Bombay Government. But the English community was divided into three parties: one who paid their court to Spencer, the rising sun; another gratefully adhered to Crommelin; and the third was affectionately devoted to the interest of Hodges, whom they considered to have been deprived of his just right as successor to Crommelin. Crommelin had gone out as a writer to Bombay in 1732, Hodges in 1737 and Spencer in 1741.

At that time supercession in the Company's service was little known; faithful service and a fair character, if life was spared, generally met with reward. Previous to Lord Clive being appointed Governor of Bengal, in 1764, Spencer had been removed from Bombay to Calcutta, and for some time he had acted as the Provisional Governor of Bengal. On Lord Clive's nomination to the Government of Bengal, Spencer was appointed by the court of directors to return to Bombay, with the rank of second in council, and an order to succeed Mr. Crommelin in January 1767. This supercession and appointment was deemed an act of injustice by the Company's civil servants in general, and as personal injury by Mr. Hodges in particular, who was then Chief of Surat, second in council, and next in regular succession to the Government of Bombay, which he looked upon as his right, being senior to Mr. Spencer by four years.

In his frustration Hodges addressed a spirited letter from Surat to the Governor and Council, complaining of injustice in the court of directors, with whom, as an individual, he was not permitted to correspond. The Governor and Council of Bombay deeming his letter improper, and disrespectful to his employers, ordered him to reconsider it, and make a suitable apology; this not being complied with, he was removed from his post as Chief of Surat, and suspended from the Company's service.

The learned brahmin knew Hodges from his younger days in the service and they were good friends. The brahmin had assured Hodges that he would gradually rise from the station he then held at Cambay, to other higher appointments as Chief at Tellicheny and Surat, and would close his Indian career by being Governor of Bombay.

Hodges spoke of these brahminical predictions among his associates and friends from their very first communication; and their author was generally called Mr. Hodges' brahmin. However, these predictions for some years made but little impression on Hodges' mind. Afterwards, as he successively ascended the gradations in the Company's service, he placed more confidence in his brahmin, especially when he approached near the pinnacle of ambition and found himself Chief of Surat, the next situation in wealth and honour to the Governorship of Bombay. When, therefore, Spencer was appointed Governor and Hodges suspended from service, he sent for his brahmin and told him about his situation and impending departure for England. He even slightly reproached him for having deceived him by false promises. The brahmin coolly replied, "You see this veranda, and the apartment to which it leads; Mr. Spencer has reached the portico, but he will not enter the palace. He has set his foot upon the threshold, but he shall not enter into the house! Notwithstanding all appearances to the contrary, you will attain the honours I foretold, and fill the high station to which he has been appointed. A dark cloud is before him!"

This singular prophecy was publicly known in Surat and Bombay; and the truth or falsehood of the brahmin was the subject of discussion in every company. Hodges' faith in his prediction seemed to have very little influence on his conduct; for, in obedience to the orders of his superiors, he had returned from Surat to Bombay, and was preparing for his voyage to Europe. Then suddenly in November 1766, an express communication arrived from England via the overland route and then by sea from Basra to Bombay. There was a letter from the court of directors to the President and Council, in answer to their representation about Hodges' conduct, mentioning, in the first place, that on a review of Spencer's proceedings while he was the Governor of Bengal, he appeared so blameable that they had thought proper to annul his appointment to the Government of Bombay, to dismiss him from the Company's service, and order him to proceed to England without delay.

Although the conduct of Mr. Hodges had been improper they were pleased to pass it over; and, in consideration of his long and faithful services, his good character and well-known abilities, they had taken off his suspension, and ordered him to succeed to the Government of Bombay on Mr. Crommelin's transfer in the month of January 1767. So, Spencer embarked for England finally in

December; and Mr. Crommelin sailed in January, leaving Hodges in complete possession of the Government. Thereafter Hodges developed such a deep faith and respect for his brahmin friend that as the Governor of Bombay he undertook no important step without consulting him.

The second episode relates to the same brahmin and was as well-known in Bombay as the former. When Forbes first arrived in Bombay to join as a writer in the Company, he met a very kindhearted gentleman who introduced him to his family and treated him as one of his family members. The lady of the house had been a widow when she had married this gentleman. Her first husband had died when she was very young, leaving two children, a son and a daughter. The latter remained with her mother, the former was sent to England for education, and at the age of sixteen embarked for Bombay with the appointment of a writer, some years prior to Forbes' arrival there. The ships of that season all reached Bombay in safety, except the one in which this young gentleman sailed, which at length was taken as lost.

A mother could not so easily give up hope and her usual evening walk was on a sandy beach, forming a bay in full view of the ocean. The shore of that bay was also a cremation place for the Hindus where brahmins assembled for the ceremony, and Hodges' brahmin, then at Bombay, was occasionally among them.

Observing the mother's anxiety, he asked her the cause; the lady being a native of India, inquired in his own language why a man so extraordinarily gifted should be ignorant of her sad situation. The brahmin was moved and said, "I do know the reason of your sorrow; your son lives; the ship will soon arrive in safety, but you will never more behold him!" She immediately mentioned this conversation to her friends. A signal was given to locate the missing ship. It was traced but her son had remained in Brazil, where the ship having been long detained for repair, the Jesuits had converted this promising youth to the church of Rome. Instead of conducting him to his mother, they only delivered her letters full of affectionate entreaties that she should follow his example, and enter into the true church. Her son stayed on at Rio de Janeiro, and occasionally wrote to her, but after the suppression of the Jesuits with many other members of that society, he was sent from South America to the prisons of Portugal, and no more heard of.

His sister, who remained with her mother at Bombay married a gentleman in the Company's civil service, by whom she had a large family. Her sudden demise in England where she had gone to supervise the education of her children brought another terrible blow to the mother. Not long after this event, an intimate friend of the family on a visit to Lisbon found the long lost son in a prison there. The information about the young man was conveyed to London immediately and official steps were taken to restore the young man to his mother. This extraordinary news did shed a momentary gleam of joy on her countenance, but it was soon succeeded by renewed pangs of sorrow, and a continued exclamation of "O the Brahmin! The Brahmin!"

Her husband endeavoured to rouse her from melancholy by assurances that every difficulty was removed, that the Almighty having infinite wisdom thought proper to deprive her of one child, had mercifully restored another in this unexpected manner, whom she had long considered dead. All seemed to produce no effect, even on a religious mind, of which resignation and indifference seemed to have taken mingled possession. Every prospect set before her of future joy and comfort only produced a monotonous repetition of "The Brahmin! The Brahmin!"

The friend at Lisbon, when all was happily accomplished, lost no time in communicating to her son that his mother lived, was married to a gentleman of fortune and respectability, and both were waiting to welcome him under their parental roof and that he had come to take him from a scene of misery to life, light, and joy.

Although the communication was made in the most considerate manner, the sudden transition seemed too much for human nature. The son's spirit failed, for he believed it not or scarcely believed the reality of his emancipation from those dreary walls where he had for years been debarred from the light of the sun and fresh air. The sudden transition from hopeless despair in the dungeon's gloom to the sight of the sun, the fanning of the breeze, and the sympathy of friendship, were too much for his emaciated frame. He faintly uttered the effusions of a grateful heart, and expired. Thus was the brahmin's prediction to his mother, uttered a full thirty years before, completely fulfilled.

The third episode refers to a young gentleman and his wife with a child who arrived in Bombay from England. Having been appointed to a Company's post at Surat, he proceeded there leaving his wife with a friend's family until he had procured a house, and made suitable provisions for her reception at Surat. On the eve of her departure for Surat, the same brahmin astrologer happened to visit her host family in Bombay. The host who was holding a high position introduced him to the company, and in a sort of jest asked him to tell the destiny of the happy, fair one lately arrived from Europe. To the surprise of the whole company, and particularly to the surprise of the object of inquiry, he gave her a penetrating and compassionate look; and after a solemn pause, said to the gentleman in the native language, "Her cup of felicity is full, but evanescent. A bitter potion awaits her; for which she must prepare."

Her husband had written that he would come in a barge to Surat to accompany her on shore. He did not appear; but a friend of his went on board to inform her of his dangerous illness; he was then in the last paroxysm of a fever, and expired in her arms.

Forbes after citing these cases pays tribute to the ancient wisdom of "Hindustan, where arts and science, learning and philosophy and the sublimest poetry, were encouraged by the native sovereigns at a time when Greece and Rome were involved in darkness, and Egypt herself was probably in a state of comparative barbarism." He adds: "The Mahomedan conquests and other causes have sadly degraded not only the philosophy and science of the Hindoos, but totally destroyed the simplicity of a religion which there can be no doubt was then essentially different from modern brahminism. If there should still remain any of that priesthood who adore God in his unity, and cherish the sublime ideas then inculcated, it is perhaps not easy to determine the limits of their researchers, or the gifts and talents they possess."

Sahib's Fancy for the Hookah

When the British came as traders, the Mughals and their Persian culture dominated the Indian scene. The early settlers were greatly influenced by the Indian lifestyle and adopted local customs and habits in respect of food and dress. There was no colour prejudice and marriages with native women were common and even encouraged by the East India Company. In the field of recreation and amusement, the British became more Indianised as we find them riding out for shikar, enjoying

John Wombell, the Company's accountant, Lucknow by a local artist, c. 1785

nautch parties, playing chess, and smoking the hookah. In fact they tried to adopt any Indian fashion or custom which made life more delicious and enjoyable.

The Indian hookah is described as an elegant and expensive equipage of a very complex form consisting of five individual components – the hookah bottom serving as a water reservoir, a snake or tube, a mouth piece, an earthen *chillum* and a silver cover which fitted the rim of the *chillum*. The pleasure of hookah smoking seems to have found favour with some early English merchants as references to the hookah can be found in the *Factory Miscellaneous Records* of 1675. Company inventories too reveal the dominance of the hookah.

Hookah smoking thus became a favourite past time by the middle of the 18th century and contemporary Raj literature carries interesting information about this luxurious habit which required an employment of a special servant, the *hookah burdar*, whose duty it was to be in readiness with his master's hookah and all its accompaniments in perfect order whenever he may be called for, and particularly after meals.

When dinner was removed, the *hookah burdar* entered the room with the prepared and lighted hookah, which he placed behind his master's chair on a small mat or stand, presented him with the snake (flexible tube), and with a phial of rose water from his girdle, a small quantity of which, poured through the mouth piece, imparted additional freshness to the smoke of the *chillum* as it passed through. He then took his station behind the hookah which he attentively watched and kept in order with his tongs, taking care also in due time to prepare a fresh *chillum* in another surpooce, and when his master said, *"doosera chillum laow"* (bring another *chillum*), to be quick in replacing the old one with it.

The most unpleasant element of the hookah was the loud rattling of water, caused by the quick passage of the tobacco smoke through it. In large parties this produced a loud concert and the violent snoring noises presented a strange spectacle to newcomers.

The popularity of the hookah extended even to the Governor General's palace at Calcutta as seen from the following invitation issued from the Government House in 1779:

> "Mr. and Mrs. Hastings present their compliments to Mr. ... and request the favour of his company to a concert and supper on Thursday next. Mr. ... is requested to bring no servants except his hookah burdar."

This invitation also shows that even the first lady of Calcutta was indulgent to the practice of hookah smoking. The fashion of hookah smoking was so well established that even memsahibs had got addicted to it. The nautch, rice pullao and curry, chewing of pan and the hookah were all part of the same culture.

Grand Pre, the French traveller who visited Calcutta in 1789 gives the following account in his journal: "Every *hookah burdar* prepares separately that of his master in an adjoining apartment and entering all together with the dessert they range themselves round the table. For half an hour there is a continued clamour, and nothing is distinctly heard but the cry for silence, till the noise subsides and the conversation assumes its usual tone. It is scarcely possible to see through the cloud of smoke, which fills the apartment. The effect produced by these circumstances is whimsical enough to a stranger and if he has not his hookah he will find himself in an awkward and unpleasant situation. The rage of smoking extends even to the ladies, and the highest compliment they can pay a man is to give him preference by smoking his hookah. In this case it is a point of politeness to take off a mouthpiece he is using and substitute a fresh one, which he presents to the lady with his hookah who soon returns it. This compliment is not always of trivial importance, it sometimes signifies a great deal to a friend, and often still more to a husband."

At formal dinners, the hookahs were placed before the invited guests. Stavorinus writes about a dinner given to a Dutch director in Bengal when silver hookahs were placed before each of the company. The luxury of hookah smoking consisted not only in the fine quality and frequent washings of the tobacco, but also mixing with it dried fruits, the conserve of roses, sweet herbs, spices, and a variety of fragrant ingredients. The sweet-smelling smoke was then inhaled from the snake or flexible tube eight or ten feet in length and drawn through the rose water in the hookah bottom, which remained at a pleasant temperature.

Hookah burdar by B. Solvyns, Calcutta, c. 1800

The British nabobs of the day watched nautches and enjoyed Persian poetry while the hookah snakes encircled their waists as they puffed through the gold or ivory mouthpieces.

The hookah was considered not only fashionable but also an indispensable article in the dining room of every house of the affluent and respectable sahibs. Also the hookah rug constituted one of the fancy carpet pieces which was often presented to friends and relatives on special occasions. The hookahs added glamour to dinner parties when they were brought in at a specified time. One could then witness sometimes thirty hookahs on each side of the table, one behind almost every diner. The gargle of these sixty hookahs produced a strange and rather discordant music, but no dinner would have been rated complete and elegant without these grand hookahs.

The exotic cloudy scene is aptly described in the following lines composed by a contemporary resident of Calcutta:

> *What is it through halls magnificently long*
> *Rolls the thick clouds and tunes the hollow song,*
> *Tis thou O Hookah! source of calm delight!*
> *Oft grasped at morn, and played upon till night.*

The ultimate luxury of smoking the hookah was to take its puffs while enjoying palanquin travel, the most popular mode of conveyance in those days. As the bearers carried their master in the palanquin, the *hookah burdar* would run alongside carrying the hookah in full operation.

The etiquette of smoking a hookah in those days demanded that one should never step over another's hookah snake. It was considered a great insult and many duels were fought over it to save the hookah's honour.

The wealthy sahibs' fancy for their hookahs inspired them to have their hookah bottoms made of silver and gold studded with precious stones, with their own monograms. Also available were beautiful cut glass of British manufacture, but the most common hookah bottoms were of black metal inlaid with silver. The snake was composed of a light brass or silverware spirally twisted and then finished with a covering of fine silk or brocade ornamented with gold or silver at the head and tail. The mouthpiece was a symbol of one's wealth and so was made either of solid gold, silver, agate or ivory. The tobacco mixture was also specially prepared by adding dried fruits, conserve of roses, and a variety of fragrant ingredients, and then matured by keeping it underground in earthen jars underground for a few weeks.

The hookahs were of different designs and names. In Bombay, hookahs were known as "Cream Cans" apparently named after Karim Khan Zend, the King of South Persia who had reportedly invented it. Another type was the "Ailoon," which was also of Persian origin. The poor man's hookah was called the "Hubble-Bubble." Another variety is mentioned as the "Kalyan" – a western hookah with a large bottom. In Surat, hookahs were called "Nargils" and in Calcutta a small hookah used by common folk was called "Goorgore." It was, however, in Lucknow and in the other princely state of Rajasthan that the hookah was seen in all its splendour and embellishment.

Hookah smoking was universal among the sahibs and memsahibs of Bombay and Calcutta. Emily Eden, sister of Governor General Auckland noted in 1837 that "aide-de-camps and doctors get their newspapers and hookah" in the morning.

But later, as the 19th century rolled on, hookah smoking began to decline. A hookah was more expensive than a cigar or a pipe because besides the cost of rose water and tobacco it also required a special servant to service it. The new arrivals found it an expensive luxury, which not many of them could easily afford. So hookah smoking fell into bad days, and Sir Charles Doyley in *The European in India* notes that not one in three were then smokers although the custom had been almost universal. Later there were opponents of the custom who condemned hookah smoking in the columns of the Calcutta press, but the custom did not go away so easily and it came to light that some old gentlemen took their hookahs to England and one lady is said to have used it in Scotland for many years. While the custom vanished in the Presidency towns, it lingered on in other parts of the country until the middle of the 19th century when it was replaced by the cheroot and the cigar.

The Great Rope and Other Tricks

The most amazing and mind-boggling tricks and feats are said to have been performed by Indian jugglers. European accounts refer at length to these performances, including the famous rope trick, and other feats of legerdemain unknown in the West. The foreigners were so completely wonder struck after seeing these performances that some of them attributed mysterious and supernatural powers to the jugglers.

The most controversial and mysterious of all was the legendary Indian rope trick. It finds a

Man showing levitation by John Gantz, c. 1820

mention in the *Jatakas* and also in the commentary on the *Mandukya Upanishad*. Shankaracharya speaks of "the magician, *the mayavin* who throws a cord up into the air, and armed, climbs up it, beyond the range of sight, to enter into battle and be dismembered; after his bodily parts have fallen to the ground, he is seen to rise up again and there is no concern over thinking about the reality of the magic trick that has been performed."

A somewhat similar description of this miraculous feat is found in Sir Henry Yule's account of Marco Polo who had heard or seen it. Another popular version of this trick is attributed to Ibn Batuta who witnessed it in Delhi in the 14th century. Then in the 17th century there is a graphic account of the rope trick in the memoirs of Jehangir who witnessed the performance at his court. By the end of the 19th century, newspapers both in India and abroad were carrying reports by travellers who claimed to have witnessed the rope trick. The London *Morning Post* carried the testimony of Sir Ralph Pearson, Lieutenant Governor of the North West Frontier Province (NWFP) who had seen the rope trick in the West Khandesh district of Bombay. Lord Fredrick Hamilton, who thought he had seen the trick, concluded that it was the result of many *salaams* that the magician executed, thereby producing a drugged audience or mass hypnosis, which helped the legend live.

There were others who dismissed it both as a miracle and as a trick. Some others held that the trick was indeed performed, not just as a miracle but as an artful illusion.

Finally, the mystery of the trick was unravelled by A. C. Brown in his interesting book, *The Ordinary Man's India* (1927). "The Rope trick," he writes, "is more talked about than seen. But nevertheless there is a certain amount of truth in the story of this Eastern magic."

He cites the evidence of three Europeans, all of whom had actually seen the trick with their own eyes. The first is Lady Waghorn who had seen it near Madras in 1892 and wrote in *The Daily Mail* testifying to its genuineness. She describes how standing about fifteen feet from the magician, she saw a fairly stout rope thrown up about twelve feet into the air. It became rigid, and a boy of about twelve climbed up and vanished at the top. A few minutes later he reappeared in the branches of a mango tree in the garden a hundred yards away.

The second testimony was given to the author by Mr. Bodalin, a Dutchman living in Calcutta, who witnessed it on the maidan. His experience was similar to that described by Lady Waghorn, save only that after the boy had apparently ascended the rigid rope, the magician himself ran up the rope and shouted to the boy to come down. There was no reply, so the magician in a rage whipped out a knife and slashed it wildly above his head. When he slid down the rope, the knife in his hand was dripping with what appeared to be blood. Soon thereafter, the boy appeared, forcing his way to the centre from the outskirts of the crowd.

Next, he relates the testimony of Colonel Bernard, the Commissioner of Police in Calcutta, which really solves once and for all the mystery of the rope trick. The Colonel was invited to attend a private performance of the rope trick in an Indian house. He asked another police officer to accompany him, and managed to take a small camera unobserved. While the performance was going on, the Colonel managed to secure several snapshots of the proceedings. He saw the boy climb the rope and disappear, large as life, and stand again by the side of the conjurer. He was frankly amazed, and said so; but when he developed the negatives he found the camera had not seen as much as its master. There was the boy and the conjurer, but the rope was on the ground at the very moment when the Colonel had seen it in the air. And the boy also was on the ground – shown clearly on each negative. The author concludes that as the camera cannot lie, its evidence had to be believed, so the only explanation possible is that the whole affair was an optical illusion.

Another very popular show reported from the 17th century onwards was the mango trick. Here the juggler would plant a mango stone in the ground and show at brief intervals the plant rising above the ground and successively producing leaves, flowers and fruit as he continued with his incantations. Both J. B. Tavernier and Francois Bernier describe this trick. So also does the Reverend Ovington (1688) who believed that it was due to black magic, because a gentleman became ill after eating one of the mangoes, and did not recover until, following a brahmin's advice, he restored the mango stone to the juggler.

An English chaplain, on seeing the trick, protested against Christians witnessing such shows, which involved the display of non-Christian powers.

Jugglers and acrobats from Rousselet's 'India and its Native Princes'

Another trick, considered by Europeans as unprecedented in the annals of jugglery, was the basket trick involving the mysterious disappearance of a girl. It was an instance of visual illusion and appeared to contain an element of the marvellous. The Reverend Caunter in his journal (1834) gives a vivid description of this trick. Under a wicker basket the juggler placed a small girl about eight years old. When she was properly secured, he asked her some questions, which she instantly answered; and the voice appeared to come so distinctly from the basket, that there was no deception. They held a conversation for some moments, then the juggler seized a sword and plunged it through, withdrawing it several times and repeating the plunge with all the blind ferocity of an excited demon. Reverend Caunter writes: "The blood ran in streams from the basket; the child was heard to struggle under it; her groans fell horridly upon the ear; her struggles smote painfully upon the heart. The former were gradually subdued into a faint moan and the latter into a slight rustling sound; we seemed to hear the last convulsive gasp which was to set her innocent soul free from the gored body, when to our inexpressible astonishment and relief, after muttering a few cabalistic words, the juggler took up the basket, but no child was to be seen. The spot was indeed dyed with blood but there were no mortal remains, and after a few moments of undissembled wonder, we perceived the little object of our alarm coming towards us among the crowd. She advanced and saluted us, holding out her hand for our donations, which we bestowed with hearty good will. What rendered the deception the more extraordinary was that the man stood aloof from the crowd during the whole performance – there was not a person within several feet of him."

The French traveller, Louis Rousselet (1860s), who also witnessed the basket trick noted that it was one of the most curious tricks of the East.

Another amazing feat, which bewildered spectators, was the swallowing of a sword blade apparently at the risk of one's life. It is described at great length by James Forbes in his *Oriental Memoirs* (1813): "Seating himself the juggler took the sword, which had a straight blade, about twenty-six inches in length and one in breadth, with edges and point blunted, and after oiling it, he introduced the point into his mouth and pushed it gently down his throat." Until the hand of Forbes, who held the hilt, came in contact with his lips. "He then made a sign to me," says the writer, "with one of his hands, to feel the point of sword between his breast and navel, which I could plainly do by bending him a little more backwards, and pressing my fingers on his stomach." On withdrawing the blade, blood was seen on some parts of it.

Sir Thomas Munro in his narrative (c.1810) mentions that the juggler, after showing his skill with the sword blade, swallowed a complete horse's tail about two feet long, introducing it into his mouth by the lower end, and gorging it to the very stump, without distorting a feature in his face, though the uneven hairs must have pricked his throat as they descended.

Egg dance by a woman performer by Emile Bayard, c. 1870

Henry Grose in his journals (1750-64) gives another astonishing story of the jugglers and pays tribute to their humane approach and compassion. "A long boat with men going from an English ship to Calcutta, a fortified settlement we have on the banks of the Ganges in Bengal, stopped short of it a considerable way, waiting for the return of the tide, and went on short to a Moorish village, where just at that time were some of the jugglers showing to a mob gathered round them their various tricks; one of which, and no juggle, was the firing of a pistol loaded with powder down one of their throats. On the arrival of the sailors, this was to be repeated, for they had before done it; but their powder having been consumed, one of the sailors offered the man some he had about him. It was accepted and the effect of it was that being much stronger than what they used for this purpose, it killed the man upon the spot. As he was a Mahometan, and the whole village was so, the mob instantly rose, and were preparing to massacre all the sailors there, in revenge for the Mussulman's blood and would infallibly have done so, but for the humane interposition of the jugglers themselves, who declared, that however sorry they might be for the death of their brother, it was no means imputable to the English, who were evidently clear of any malicious design in it. This alone appeased the populace and the sailors were suffered to return quietly to their boat."

Levitation shows have also been recorded by many travellers during this time. The serial suspension was performed in 1820s in Madras by an old brahmin, Seshal, "with no better apparatus than a piece of plank, which with four legs, he formed into an oblong stool; and upon which, in a little brass socket, he placed in a perpendicular position, a hollow bamboo, from which projected a kind of crutch, covered with a piece of common hide – he was seen poised in the air about four feet from the ground in a sitting attitude, the outer end of one hand merely touching the crutch, with fingers deliberately counting beads, and the other hand and arm held up in an erect posture."

In 1875, Harry Keller, in the company of the Prince of Wales witnessed levitation in the maidan of Calcutta. It was believed that some Indian yogis, through spiritual means, could defy physical laws.

Among other clever tricks, there are descriptions of jugglers changing pebbles into birds, birds into eggs and eggs into plants; they would thread beads with their tongues, join innumerable pieces of cotton into one long cord, keep half a score of sharp knives in the air at once, throw cannon balls with their toes, spin tops on the ends of twigs and make rings and coins move about on the ground with a kind of dancing or jerking motion. One of the favourite tricks was to borrow a watch and transport it to some unthought of place and send the owner to find it. There are authentic accounts of all these tricks by those who witnessed

Juggler swallowing a sword blade by Charles Gold, c. 1790

these shows. In 1814, a party of Indian jugglers consisting of two men and a boy were taken to England from Madras by the captain of the *Monarch*. They demonstrated their art at Pall Mall three times a day and created a sensation. They jolted the English artistes who could only manage leaping and rope dancing.

As regards feats of manual skill, Indians were considered unequalled in the world. Their physical strength too was perfectly amazing considering their simple diet and the climate in which they lived. Among their extraordinary feats may be mentioned somersaults and capers made with wonderful agility, crossing elephants and camels, jumping through a frame supporting a dozen cut glasses and many other arduous exercises requiring extreme caution and delicacy.

The skill and strength displayed by women was equally dazzling. Dr. Fryer saw a woman who held nine gilded balls in play with her hands and feet and the muscles of the arms and legs, for a long time together without letting them fall. J. D. Gay, special correspondent of the *Daily Telegraph* who accompanied the Prince of Wales in 1875 speaks about "a stout girl who threw a man weighing eleven stones over her shoulders, then seizing him once more, placing him crossways on her back and tossing him into the air as though he were made of feathers and was not a broad-shouldered human being. Turning backwards on her feet she picked up straws with her eyelids, threw somersaults and lifted weights which would have astonished any London acrobat. There were also little girls rolling themselves into balls, tying themselves into knots, going through a bewildering amount of dislocation, and with their eyes bandaged, threading a needle with their toes."

Among other street performers were the *bazigars* or acrobats who performed stunts such as dancing on long stilts, climbing and balancing poles. A real delight for European children was the *katpootliwallah* or the puppet player. The comedy played by him was mainly a procession of rajas who entered two and two in a durbar but there was an undercurrent of farce which gave some life to the exhibition. There would be a comic scene of a wayfarer being robbed by a thief and bullied by a policeman, a satirical character. The sahibs engaged them to present special shows for the amusement of their children.

Finally, there was the common *bunderwallah* who roamed about town with three or four monkeys and a goat. He made them dance to the beat of his hand drum and performed several wonderful tricks with the goat which also served as a mount for the monkeys. The monkeys also performed many laughable tricks at the bidding of the *bunderwallah*.

It is a pity that many of the skills of Indian jugglers and other street performers have long disappeared from the scene. As is well known, the Indian art of jugglery was handed down from father to son and it was always a well-guarded secret in a family. In the course of time, performers died without imparting the secret of their art to anyone. But for the detailed accounts left behind by foreign visitors and sketches by European artists, we would have remained ignorant about some of the wonderful feats of our performing artistes.

Shikar and Animal Fights

The English sahibs were introduced to big game hunting by Indian Rajas and Nawabs for whom it had been a traditional outdoor sport from time immemorial. Over the years, as the East India Company acquired power and prestige, shikar (hunting) emerged as the most popular and adventurous sport both for civilians and soldiers. By the beginning of the 19th century, it dominated their outdoor life and no other subject occupies a more

A battle between a buffalo and a tiger by Samuel Howitt, c. 1820

prominent place in Raj literature than shikar. There are countless accounts of hunting expeditions with stories of adventurous encounters with wild animals, including tigers, leopards, lions, hogs, and wild buffaloes.

The manly ideal of the 19th century with its stress on physical prowess expected an Englishman to be a good shot and a good rider. The Raj accepted this manly ideal as the right way for an Englishman to conduct himself both at work and play. English sportsmen in their lively accounts seem to take the readers with them on their hunting trips and introduce them to the sights, sounds, and hazards of the sport. They bring alive the world of animals in the vast jungles of India from Mysore to the Himalayas.

Amongst the many books written on the subject, perhaps the most comprehensive and informative is *Forty Years Among the Wild Animals of India* by F. C. Hicks of the Imperial Forest Service. The incidents narrated by him are the pick of his experiences of a long period spent almost entirely in pursuit of big game in dense jungles. It is both a scientific study and a guide for sportsmen.

Hicks evolved an assiduous and systematic approach to hunting in order to outwit the most cunning of all animals – an experienced old tiger. He observes, "I have a vague idea of trying on occasions to count up and accounting for over 200 tigers which I have shot, but whether those were all of them, or only half, I could not say in the least." Laced with anecdotes about the behaviour of animals, he gives details about locations and actual encounters with ferocious wild animals.

Hunting remained one of the favourite pastimes and principal diversions of the Englishmen throughout the Raj. It was also considered an essential exercise to enhance the Imperial image. Pigsticking and tiger shooting were the first two sports full of excitement and danger. Tiger hunts were grand affairs with dozens of elephants and a big base camp.

The game of games, easily the most popular however, with both civilians and soldiers was pigsticking, or hog-hunting according to Bombay phraseology. It was at the beginning of the 19th century that pigsticking was recognised as a substitute for bearsticking, which had till then been the most popular sport of Bengal. The classic centres of this sport were Bengal and the North West Provinces (UP) and to a lesser extent, Bombay. Madras offered bison

Col. Mordaunt's cock fight match at Lucknow by John Zoffany, 1786

and buffalo while in Assam there were rhinoceros, but none of these beasts called for those qualities required for the pursuit of the boar.

Pigsticking was considered an ideal manly activity requiring strength, toughness, and quick wit. From the Governor General to the district officer, everyone found it the most exciting and adventurous of field sports. It is recorded that M. Elphinstone, the Governor of Bombay, would take his whole staff out for hog-hunting. Daniel Johnson in his *Sketches of Indian Field Sports* (1827) gives a detailed description of the methods used for hunting wild boars, instructions for the use of spears, best horses for pigsticking and how to manage them when hunting. He also points out the dangers and difficulties involved in the game and explains the techniques of surmounting all kinds of problems as well as necessary precautions for hunters in the different seasons of the year. The account is supplemented with a great many anecdotes of hogs and hog-hunters.

Captain Williamson in his classic *Oriental Field Sports* (1819) gives a vivid description of hog-hunting expeditions and the courage and ferocity of the boars. Besides anecdotes, he offers advice to the hunters on "how to succeed as a pigsticker."

Captain R. S. S. Baden-Powell was an authority on the subject. In his book *Pigsticking* (1889), a complete guide for pigstickers, he compares the game to a battlefield as both "demand the dash and keenness, the pluck and determination for ultimate victory." Another contemporary writer proclaimed hog-hunting as "the most entertaining, noble and manly of all sports; the best school for young cavalry officers. They learn to ride better from one day's keen hog-hunting than from a year's exercise with their regiment." To quote another supporter of pigsticking: "The training that makes a sportsman makes a soldier; it gives him endurance and it gives him an eye for a country and familiarity with danger."

Civilian officers were also encouraged to take to pigsticking as they had huge responsibilities in the districts and much loneliness. Pigsticking helped them preserve their sanity and sense of proportion. Anyone engaged in pigsticking had to be an excellent horseman, have the power of quick and cool judgement, and a determination not to be beaten. These qualities were also needed for a good administrator. It was pointed out by a votary of the sport that "the danger and excitement, the ferocity thus harmlessly given an outlet, sweetened men who might otherwise have been soured by files and hot weather and disappointment, as lime sweetens grass soured by poultry. Ugly lusts for power and revenge melted away and even the lust for women assumed, so it was said, reasonable proportions after a day in pursuit of a pig."

Edward Bradden, another champion propagandist of pigsticking, in his famous book, *Thirty years of Shikar* (1895) offers a graphic account of this exciting sport and practical guidelines for the novice to avoid accidents. "I have seen some accidents," he writes, "from mismanagement of the spear. I have seen a man heavily thrown as a consequence of his running his spear into the ground; I have seen a rider spear his own horse and that of his companion; and any one of these accidents may occur to the novice or to him who is inexpert or careless." He adds, "A boar in its prime is no mean foe ... quick and intrepid in attack, each charge it makes home to its object may leave a wound in horse or rider, and it is like an Englishman in that it does not know when it is beaten."

Another fascinating account of pigsticking comes from a sportswoman, Isabel Savory, who was thrilled by this hair-raising sport. "Pigsticking is always wildly exciting," she writes. "No one

A dead tiger by Samuel Howitt, c. 1810

realises who is near, or what may be in front; it is a case of riding as never before one has ridden; and the excitement of a breakneck gallop only gives place at the finish to a battle royal, fraught with danger."

From later accounts, we find that the Indian princes and Nawabs patronised these sports on festive occasions and held special shows to entertain the British elite. Captain Mundy in his journal gives a graphic account of a series of animal fights organised in 1827 by the King of Oudh in honour of the Commander-in-Chief Lord Cambermere in Lucknow. "A gigantic cage of strong bamboos, about fifty feet high, with the same diameter and roofed with a rope network was set up in the centre. Several wild animals were kept in small cells with sliding doors opening into the main theatre. In the large cage, crowded together, and presenting a formidable front, well armed with horns, stood a group of buffaloes sternly awaiting the conflict. As soon as the trap-doors were lifted, two tigers and the same number of bears and leopards, rushed into the cage. The buffaloes instantly commenced hostilities, and made complete shuttlecocks of the bears, who however, finally escaped by climbing up the bamboos beyond the reach of their horned antagonists. The tigers, one of which was a beautiful animal, fared scarcely better; indeed, the odds were much against them, there being five buffaloes.

They appeared, however, to be no match for these powerful creatures, even single-handed, and showed little disposition to be the assaulters. The larger tiger was much gored in the head, and in return took a mouthful of his enemy's dewlap, but was finally bored to the ropes and floored. Throughout the conflict, the leopards remained on the sideline and avoided breach of peace. Thereafter, a rhinoceros was let loose in the open courtyard and the attendants tried to induce him to attack a tiger who was chained to a ring. The rhinoceros, however, considered a fettered foe as quite beneath his enmity. Having once approached the tiger, he quietly surveyed him, as he writhed and growled, expecting the attack, turned suddenly round and trotted awkwardly off to the yard gate, where he capsized a palanquin which was carrying away an English lady tired of witnessing these fearful sports.

A buffalo and a tiger were the next combatants. They attacked furiously, the tiger springing at the first onset on the other's head, and tearing his neck severely.

But he was quickly repulsed by the buffalo and thrown with such force that nearly broke his back and disabled him from renewing the combat. A small elephant was next impelled to attack a leopard. The battle was short and decisive. The elephant falling

Hunting a tiger by Samuel Howitt, c. 1810

on his knees thrusted his blunted tusks through his adversary. The concluding spectacle was of elephant fights on the sandy banks of the Goomty river. The well trained elephants, fed with exciting spices and led by two or three men armed with long spears advanced slowly from opposite sides of the plain. As they approached, their speed gradually increased, and at length they met with a grand shock, entwining their trunks, until one, finding himself overmatched, turned tail, and received his adversary's charge in the rear. This was so violent, that the mahout of the flying elephant was dislodged from his seat but fortunately he escaped with a few bruises."

Tigers were often pitted against leopards but the leopards were so powerful that the tigers could hardly ever beat them. Even camels were made to fight each other when excited. The common people enjoyed watching fights between rams, who were trained for combat by the butchers and some lower classes.

When Lord William Bentinck, the Governor General visited Lucknow in 1831, several animal fights were organised for his entertainment. Fanny Parks in her famous journal describes some of them. "Two male elephants were brought in the arena and a female one placed midway. This inflamed the males who attacked each other with their tusks. They seized each other with their long trunks and interlocked them. When the fight grew fierce, fireworks were thrown to separate them." She adds that the king had also arranged a fight between two tigers and a horse, who had the distinction of having killed two tigers earlier.

A fascinating account of a battle between a buffalo and tiger is given by Captain Thomas Williamson in his book *Oriental Field Sports* (1808). "The buffalo usually came out to fight with utmost confidence, conscious of his own prowess. With rapid and furious motions, he would charge the tiger giving it no respite and carry out a war of extermination. It was said that the buffalo would never quit until a tiger's death proclaimed his victory. In very rare instances, the tiger ever came out triumphant." Reverend Caunter who witnessed quite a few animal combats relates a scenario when an elephant fought with three buffaloes and after a long struggle crushed them to death. He also describes fights between two alligators, a leopard and an alligator, a rhinoceros and a buffalo and three wild dogs and a bear. As a missionary, he considered such fights as cruel exhibitions, which caused more distress than enjoyment to spectators. However, not many European guests who enjoyed these spectacles shared his opinion. Native rulers, on the other hand, treated animal fights as an amusing pageant to illustrate the art of war, which aroused the warrior spirit

Then there were also bird fights for entertainment. *Murghabazi* or cock-fight was the most popular pastime of the royalty, nobility and commoners alike. Lucknow was the centre of this sport. Even some Europeans living in Lucknow became its devotees and participated in cock-fights with the princes and nobles. General Claude Martin was an expert at cock fighting and Nawab Sadat Ali Khan used to bet his cocks against those of the General. Colonel John Mordaunt, Commander of Nawab Asif-ud-daula's bodyguards and a leader of the court revels, was a specialist in the sport and regularly organised cock fights for the Nawab attended by the local European gentry. Lord Hastings is reported to have attended Mordaunt's cock-fight in April 1784. The cocks were trained and made to fight with spurs and feet as well as their beaks that were specially sharpened by their trainers. When the two cocks were released in the cockpit, their masters stood behind inciting and encouraging them with cries like, "Well done my boy, bravo! Pick him, my beauty!" and "go in again." On hearing these words the cocks attacked each other with greater fury as if they understood the language of their owners. The fight ended when one of the two got blinded or disabled.

From Arrack to Whisky

Among the early English settlers, everyone from the Governors to factors and soldiers enjoyed drinks and many of them were addicted to excessive drinking. Alcohol provided an escape from boredom and loneliness and helped to stimulate their spirits and general attitude towards life. Even at the beginning of the 17th century Sir Thomas Roe found frequent bouts of drunkenness at most of the English tables. Drinking was considered as one of the "rational amusements" with which they sought to beguile time, with

Drinking in a prison cell by Rowlandson, Bombay, c. 1810

the income of the drinker determining not only the quantity but also the quality of the drink.

The most popular and staple drink in the early days was Arrack, a term applied to a variety of common spirits. French traveller Bernier was surprised at the English liking for Arrack, which he considered very hot and penetrating like Polish brandy, made from corn. Of the two principal brands of Arrack, the one from Bengal was stronger while the other from Goa, though of better quality, was comparatively milder and was used for making yeast as well as for drinking. Captain Symson, an authority on the subject describes different kinds and uses of Arrack (1720): "It was distilled sometimes from rice, sometimes from toddy and sometimes from black sugar and water mixed with the bark of a tree called "Baboul," when it was known as 'Jagre Arrack' and was as hot as brandy and drunk in drams by Europeans."

Arrack was also credited with some medicinal properties. It was said to be good for gripes ... in the morning as laxative, in the evening as astringent. But Symson added that several Europeans "lose their lives by the immoderate use of Arrack with which once inflamed they become so restless that no place is cool enough; and therefore they lie down on the ground all night which occasions their being snatched away in a very short time."

Arrack formed the basis of punch, a word derived from the Persian *panj* or Hindi *panch*, both meaning five. Arrack also got its name from the number of its ingredients: arrack, sugar, lime juice, spice, and water. This was easily the most popular drink and became a universal favourite in the first half of the 18th century. The popularity of arrack was also attributed to the fact that it could be preserved and stored through even the hottest weather, which was not the case with wines imported from Europe. It was common for everyone to consume large quantities of punch and even Company members of the Council did so in their morning meetings regularly. Historian Cotton writes; "We may picture them, dressed in muslin shirts, pyjamas, and starched white caps sitting – with a case of good old Arrack and a goblet of water on the table – which the secretary with a skilful hand converted into punch." An English captain Farwinter of Bengal Masonic Lodge liked arrack so much that he sent a chest of the best Arrack for the use of the Grand Lodge in England. It was "Punch" that gave its name to the

Portuguese drinking taverns, which came to be called "Punch Houses."

In those early hard-drinking years, sailors and soldiers were known for their reckless drinking which swallowed most of their pay. It was even reported that captains of ships run by the East India Company made their crew drunk with spirituous liquors they trafficked in. Drunkenness was common according to early Company records of Bombay as well. Not only soldiers but even officers were addicted to excessive drinking.

There was a shocking case of one Captain Wyatt who in a drunken rage murdered a soldier with his sword, but the Company was so indulgent that they just sacked him, considering it as sufficient punishment for a gentleman. Many soldiers drank strong Portugal wines at the hottest time of the day. No wonder a number of them died of intemperance. Another ruinous drink was hot wine boiled with cloves and cinnamon, which they called burnt wine. They drank it frequently in the morning to comfort their stomachs. They did not suspect any connection between drinking and a high mortality rate.

Eighteenth century doctors considered wine as an antidote to fever in hot weather if taken in the right quantity. In Madras, alcohol was considered necessary for soldiers to counteract the ill-effects of the bad water they drank. It was also thought to be useful in enhancing the fighting spirit of the soldiers. They were given an extra allowance of Arrack before going into action and were ordered to drink it up on the day of issue. No wonder there was a contemporary saying about the people that "their lives were not worth two Monsoons." Once in Calcutta an arrack licence was withdrawn from Mr. Hundle because military men of the Company were found "continually intoxicated with liquor in his tavern."

The difficulty of growing grapes in India was an obstacle in making local wine. The East India Company later imported shiraz wine from Persia, which was much in favour. Mr. Ives writes about this (1757) saying that shiraz was supplied by the Company to its servants at the western factories and was the best he ever tasted except claret. Towards the close of the 18th century, European wines were being imported for those who could afford to pay the high prices fixed for them. Moreover punch and Arrack

The bottle and the bed scene in Calcutta, c. 1800

became less popular and gave way to Madeira and later to claret and beer.

There was also a gradual realisation that it was better to live than to drink themselves into untimely graves. Mr. Tennant recorded in 1796 that "regularity of living and temperance are much more prevalent among the present inhabitants than the first adventurers." Madeira wine was now the most popular drink. So much so that one advertiser (1790) announced the arrival of his new stock of Madeira with the following couplet:

Now drink Madeira and in scorn of knaves
Leave continental wines to conquered slaves

Large shipments of wines from England and France were now regularly arriving in Calcutta. Even the Company did a little business in Madeira. It imported a large quantity annually for the use of its servants and any surplus was sold to the public. The wine was then stored and kept by the same buyers for later sale at high profit. The favourite Madeira was said to improve in the Indian climate and it was a common practice to drink Madeira before dinner and claret with dinner and afterwards when the gentlemen would sit down to relax and easily polish off three

Soldiers party at Bobbery Hall, Bombay by Rowlandson, c. 1810

bottles of claret each. For ladies it was common to drink at least a bottle while some of them competed with men in the consumption of booze. Captain Edouard de Warren, a Frenchman who served for nine years in a British regiment in India, in his book *L' Inde Anglaise* (1843) has noted his surprise at the enormous quantity of beer and wine consumed by English women. He speaks about a lady at a dinner party who calmly disposed off a bottle and a half of very strong beer alternatively with a certain amount of Burgundy and later finished up at dessert with five or six glasses of champagne very light but very strong. The only effect this had on her was to loosen her tongue and give vivacity to her eyes.

It is interesting to note the ruling prices of wines and spirits from contemporary advertisements in the early 19th century. Madeira wine was priced at Rs. 40 for a dozen (16 years old) and Rs. 28 for a dozen (for the 7 years old). Red sparkling champagne was sold at Rs. 45 for a dozen, white at Rs. 40, port wine at Rs. 25, Gin at Rs. 15, Pale Ale at Rs. 11 and Brandy at Rs. 16. Around this time, soda water was also introduced in Calcutta, substituting the use of soda powder. It was proclaimed as a pleasant drink and a valuable remedy for indigestion, comparable in quality to that made in London. Soda water was found useful for diluting strong spirits like brandy, gin, and later whisky. Later, the importing of ice from America added another flavour to the enjoyment of drinking.

By the end of the 19th century a number of breweries were set up in different parts of India and locally produced beer, rum, gin, and whisky found their way to the market. Drinking habits and tastes of the native gentry were also transformed. Contemporary advertisements in the newspapers of metropolitan cities suggest a growing demand among the Indian gentry not only for whisky, rum, and gin, but also for exotic French wines, champagne, and cognac.

The dawn of the 20th century saw the emergence of Scotch whisky as the first choice of the connoisseurs. It was a ritual for an Englishman to have his sundowner, whisky and soda on the veranda of his bungalow. The custom was attributed to the apprehension that sunset was particularly bad for catching malaria and a strong drink taken at that time was the best antidote. There is no historical record of when and where the first cask of whisky was distilled in Scotland, but ancient Celts proclaimed it as the water of life. Its popularity soared over the centuries and it was in the 1820s that the Scottish government legalised distilleries and the production of whisky. The great popularity of Scotch whisky is attributed to the traditional skill of the Scotsmen in maturing and blending of whisky, the quality of water and the oak barrels and even the structure of the warehouses. The skilful art of blending is highly complex as the master blender has to ensure that the individual elements produce a consistent aroma and taste in the finished brand of whisky. Originally praised for its medicinal properties, it is still accepted as a blood thinner and as conducive for the functioning of the human heart.

After the first World War (1914-15), there was a boom in the popularity of whisky. It was hailed as an ideal drink for the Indian climate. A wonderful stimulant, a small dose would accomplish more than what a few glasses of wine could. G. W. Osborne, who accompanied the Governor General Auckland to Maharaja Ranjit Singh's court in 1838 gives a graphic account of the Maharaja's colourful drinking parties and his special wine extracted from raisins mixed with ground pearls. He points out that of all the European wines and spirits presented to him, whisky was the only thing that Maharaja Ranjit Singh liked. The Maharaja laughed at European wines and said that he drank for excitement, and that sooner that object was attained the better. No wonder, whisky, the queen of drinks, reigns supreme and is the most popular drink in the sub-continent.

Pran Nevil, former diplomat and UN advisor, was born and educated in Lahore. He has been engaged in the study of the social and cultural history of India for several years.

He lives in New Delhi.